PRAISES FOR

MW00800413

If the 9-5 grind has sapped your energy and you are looking for some heart pulsing adventure without the use of a defibrillator, then Master Award Winning Pilot-Captain Eddie Gantner's book: "Flying Vagabond" is what you need. <u>It will keep you riveted, chapter to chapter...</u> and happily, away from your doctor's office. It is an amazing journey of one man's dream brought to reality.

Captains Eddies trails blaze across the U.S; Europe; The Middle East; and Africa. One heart stopping exploit after another. *If I were up there in the Third Dimension and things were not going well, I would want Captain Eddie Gantner right by my side.* So, Ladies and Gentlemen: *Fasten your seatbelts, and let the journey begin.*
    – Captain William Leonardi *"Dancing Through the Maze"*.

From the big radial engine transports to private luxury jets, Captain Eddie has had one hell-of-a-ride and it's all in this book...Well, almost all!
    – Jay Malloy, Captain, Continental Airlines (Ret.)

"Flying Vagabond" puts you squarely in the cockpit with Captain Eddie and his many adventures. His love of aviation is evident in these many antidotes and his development from low time pilot flying marginal WWII equipment (read big radial engines) to international captain of state of art corporate jet aircraft is spellbinding. Few pilots would admit to many of these "adventures", but Captain Eddie allows you to sit in his "office" while he takes on weather, aircrew, aircraft and Aviation Authority (read FAA) in order to complete his missions.

I found this book to be an excellent aviation read that shows a "real life" portrait of what aviation was like in the 1960's to the early

21st century. It is a history of an OLD and BOLD (sometimes not so smart) pilot that you will find most enjoyable and very difficult to put down. ENJOY!!!

— **Doug Simpson, CDR US Navy (Ret.) F-8, Falcon**

FLYING VAGABOND

AN IMPLAUSIBLE JOURNEY OF ADVENTURE AND ADRENALINE

FLYING VAGABOND

– An Implausible Journey of Adventure and Adrenaline

Copyright © 2018 by Eddie Gantner

FIRST EDITION

ISBN: 978-0-578-43013-3

Library of Congress In Publication Data

Category: Biography, Aviation

Written by: Captain Eddie Gantner | jetdude90@gmail.com

Cover Design & Book Formatted by: Eli Blyden | www.CrunchTimeGraphics.com

Printed in the United States by: A&A Printing | www.PrintShopCentral.com

10 9 8 7 6 5 4 3 2 1

CONTENTS

FOREWORD

This is the story of a young man growing up through his share of adversity. It chronicles his early years in a home broken by divorce, his difficult school years, and his plunge into adult life via the U.S. Navy. This was followed by years of hard work, pursuing a goal possible to only a few men.

Entering his 20s, he encounters the world of work with few skills beyond persistence and endurance. Adulthood turned out to be his finest classroom. It was filled with teachers who, with intimidation, disrespect, outright fear—and occasional kindness—gradually shaped him into a respected professional.

His goal was not to find an easy job but to become a respected member of one of the most challenging professions: piloting jet-powered corporate aircraft.

Armed with a strong will, he submitted himself to the rigors of flight training, entering the profession at its lowest and most dangerous level, flying freight. In the 1950s and 60s, much airfreight was moved in old World War II aircraft—C-47s or C-46s. These were all unpressurized and therefore limited to altitudes mostly below 10,000 feet. This limitation often meant flying through the weather, rather than climbing above it, as most modern pressurized jetliners do.

A freight airline could go under overnight, throwing hundreds of employees out of work—often failing to pay for the last week's work. Long periods without work forced pilots to network actively, looking for opportunities to get just one flight, maybe a few, to tide them over.

One does not get to fly the "good" equipment without experience. This man's experience seeking a break here and there (and sometimes getting it) allowed him to eventually graduate to jet-powered aircraft. He began by flying some of the older jets—old, but jets. It was a foot in the door, and he refused to pull it out. Over a period of years, with more experience, more networking, more friends, his flying hours continued to grow with a corresponding increase in his abilities. It took several years, but eventually, he found himself flying state-of-the-art corporate jets, beginning with one of the earliest corporate jets, the Hansa Jet. This was soon replaced by four models of the Learjet, two models of the Citation Jet, six models of the Hawker Jet, two models of the Bombardier Challenger Jet, the Dassault Falcon 900, and the Dassault Falcon 50, with several hours of stick time in the Gulfstream corporate jet until the end of his active flying career.

These days, although retired from active flying, he uses his vast experience and many type ratings to teach aircraft systems ground school and operate flight simulators for a multinational flight training organization where as a certified FAA flight check airman, he administers a rigorous series of tests (simulated emergencies) for both current and prospective corporate jet captains.

I know this man's story quite well. That's because he is my brother. He has done things that are beyond anything I could ever do. Through study, determination, and sheer grit he has successfully taken a lost young man through years of genuinely world-class challenges and won repeatedly. Today, he stands as a consummate professional in his field—someone any young man could envy.

This story is truly a page-turner. Welcome aboard. Enjoy the trip!

– John Gantner, DC, Cape Coral, Florida

Every story has a beginning. Before the gates of Troy, in a particular house on the island of Ithaca, on the road to Thebes, no matter where it starts, every story has a hero. As often as not, a young man on a journey from innocence to experience. Let me introduce you!

PROLOGUE

In 1969, Ypsilanti Michigan's Willow Run Airport was the home of several cargo airlines servicing the automotive industry of Detroit with DC-3s, C-46s, DC-6/7s, Argosys (AW-650,) L-188 Lockheed Electras, and DC-8 aircraft. On any given day, except for the L-188s and DC-8s, it looked like the Berlin Airlift all over again with its WWII aircraft parked side by side filling the ramp.

My employer was Zantop International Airlines, the largest and oldest freight operator on the field, dating from the 1950s and I was a brand-new Curtis-Wright Commando C-46 captain. Cargo hauling was the primary business of the airline. Much of it involved flying automobile parts between plants located around the country. The Big Three auto companies of the day; GM, Ford, and Chrysler; were the blood that coursed through the airline's veins. Much, if not most, of the flying took place at night supplying parts for the next day's production.

Awakened by the incessant ringing of the phone, I was advised, "Get here as quickly as possible. You're number one in rotation, and we've scheduled a trip for you." It was crew dispatch.

I was not sure if I could even get to the airport as the previous evening's inclement weather had left the roads almost unnavigable. A layer of fresh snow disguised the black ice of an earlier freezing rain event. Mentioning this and the wisdom of flying in such weather was ignored. "You're the duty captain. Check with meteorology when you arrive at the airport. Get here ASAP!" The line went dead.

The drive to Willow Run was treacherous. My assigned aircraft was already being de-iced as I arrived.

Picking up my trip packet from dispatch, I discovered my trip was a round robin to Cleveland—there and back. We were to deadhead, i.e., empty, to pick up a "hot cargo" load from Cleveland's Brookpark GM plant to prevent a shutdown of the General Motors assembly line in Detroit.

The weatherman stated, "With a quick de-ice, your takeoff will be well ahead of the approaching front with its expected deteriorating weather. The front should be through the Detroit area in a few hours, just in time for your return. I expect an improvement in ceilings and visibility with frontal passage."

Armed with that bit of meteorological precognition, we made haste to depart.

My first officer, Bert Wills, was a reserve captain whose lower seniority number was all that prevented him from holding a full-time captain slot. His experience level would contribute significantly to a successful flight in these adverse conditions.

A brisk west wind blew horizontally across the field. Taxiing for takeoff the weather once again transitioned from freezing drizzle and rain to wet snow. So much for the "well ahead of the front" comment from the meteorologist. Ice was beginning to form on all aircraft surfaces despite the de-icing spray just moments before. Flight controls were quickly checked as takeoff clearance was received.

Hoping upon hope the damn thing would fly, I held the aircraft on the ground several knots beyond its normal takeoff speed. It must have worked; we were flying. After raising the gear, we were on our way to Cleveland.

"This damn window is leaking like a sieve. How's yours, Bert?"

"So far, so good. Only a few drips. Nothing major. Glad I remembered my poncho though as I already have a small puddle building on my lap."

"Yeah, me too and it's getting bigger by the minute," I said.

"Be careful moving in your seat. You might find out just how cold that water really is." He laughed,

"Bert, we're starting to get some ice on the wings. Wait for a buildup, then turn on the de-icing boots.[1] Carburetor heat is already on.

"Okay, let me give Cleveland ops a call with our ETA.

"Captain, Ops advises they are ready to load as soon as we stop on the ramp. I advised them to have a de-icing truck standing by."

"While you were talking with them, I picked up ATIS (automated terminal information service). Weather is now 200 feet overcast, one-half mile visibility. Wind is variable 240/280 degrees at 14 knots, gusting to 18 in sleet. Temp is 29F. Runway 23 ILS approach in use."

"Did they have a braking action report on the terminal weather freq?"

"Yup. You won't like it. It is not conducive to getting this big bird stopped. They're calling it fair to poor. If this waiting cargo load wasn't *hot,* I doubt they would have dispatched us until there was an improvement in the weather."

"Zantop 613Z, Cleveland approach; maintain 3000 feet until established inbound, cleared for the ILS 23 approach. Switch over to tower frequency 120.5 now."

"Thanks. Zantop 613Z. See ya."

"Cleveland tower, Zantop 613Z outer marker inbound ILS runway 23."

"Zantop 613Z Cleveland tower, wind 260 degrees @14 knots, peak gust 22. Cleared to land runway 23."

---

[1] Wing "boots" are inflatable rubber bladders that expand with air pressure breaking the leading-edge ice from the wing. It is imperative to wait for ice buildup before activating to prevent the formation of ice on the already expanded bladder, rendering them ineffective. Carburetor heat prevents ice building in the carburetor, thus starving the engines of fuel causing a shutdown of the engine or engines.

"Cleared to land runway 23, Zantop 613Z."

"Runway in sight 12 o'clock."

"Landing!"

"This beast is skidding like crazy. The crosswind isn't helping much. Braking is definitely poor."

"I love long runways." Bert sighed.

"Cleveland Ops, 613Z on your ramp in five. We will be keeping number two engine running. Have de-icing commence ASAP. Crew is staying on board."

"Weather has really turned to shit here. It is beginning to snow like hell," Bert said.

"Yeah, we need to get the hell outta here and fast!"

I never dreamed that I would one day be the pilot-in-command of a large transport category aircraft weighing several tons, plying the airways in all types of weather, incurring responsibilities never imagined! Yet, here I am and loving every minute of it. I do wonder about those moments of "stark terror" I had heard described by older, more seasoned pilots! So far, so good.

FLYING VAGABOND

AN IMPLAUSIBLE JOURNEY OF ADVENTURE AND ADRENALINE

BY 'CAPT. EDDIE GANTNER

1

THE BEGINNING!

I never really thought about becoming a pilot when I was younger. I just wanted to be grown up, and I figured the rest would take care of itself.

My brother was the guy interested in flying and aviation. He worked incessantly on building and flying model aircraft, the kind you built from scratch and flew with gasoline-powered engines.

Unlike my brother, I had no hobbies or interests in anything beyond just hanging with my friends.

I attended St. Michaels Catholic grade school in Rochester, New York. The Sisters of Notre Dame taught at St. Mikes. They were hardcore, great as teachers but stern. When needed, they never hesitated to hold a youngster back a year. We all had respect for the ever-present ruler hidden in the oversized sleeves of the nuns' habits (nuns' dresses). Looking back, I just got off on the wrong foot in school. Guess you could say I was behind the bell curve from the start. My parents' divorce while I was in first grade didn't help.

I was held back twice, in the first and fifth grades. Along about the fifth or sixth grade, I discovered girls. By the eighth grade, I was sure that I was in love with at least six of my female classmates. Of course, not one of them even knew I was alive. I was very shy, I could hardly bring myself to talk to a girl. When I tried, my tongue became tangled, stuttering mostly gibberish. They would just giggle and laugh as they walked away. I pretty much withdrew into myself.

In my teens, Mom suggested that my older brother should interest me in building and flying model airplanes. He did. It didn't work. I just wasn't interested. I passed most of my time hanging with friends, often getting into minor mischief, worrying my mother to death. Mom had remarried after her divorce. My new stepdad sometimes drank a bit more than he should, leading to some heated battles between him, Mom, and me, especially, as I grew older. The tension between my dad and me caused a good deal of grief for my mother. My dad was a good hardworking fellow when sober but worthless and argumentative when drinking.

Despite his faults and our frequent disagreements, I grew to love him very much in later years. He affected my life in many ways.

I was 14 years old when I graduated from the eighth grade, two years behind my peers. Mom was quite concerned with what she considered a lack of direction in my life. She felt unable to control me, fearing for my future. One day, she approached me with a great idea: *Why not go to Germany to attend high school?* I was stunned by this radical proposal.

Mom believed that I could benefit from some good discipline. She was worried that hanging with my friends would get me into serious trouble. Looking back, she was probably correct.

Mom had a sister and three brothers in Germany. She decided I should go to Germany, living and studying with her sister's husband, my uncle Wolf, who owned and operated a "M-A-N" diesel dealership ("**M**achinenfabrik, **A**ugsburg **N**uremberg") in Bavaria. Uncle Wolf's school accepted young apprentices, teaching them theory and practice of diesel engineering with the goal of becoming a master of the craft. I didn't want to go. Other people tried to talk

Mom out of it but to no avail. I was shipped, literally, to Germany sailing on the German cruise liner Bremen. Mom went along.

We arrived in Hamburg, Germany after 10 miserable seasick days. A swarm of relatives turned out to greet us. There was much hugging and kissing. Holy cow, who were these people? They scared me!

I had only modest German language skills. I had no idea what all these Germans were rattling on about. All I knew was that I didn't want to be there. I fought it from the first day.

The very next day I was introduced to the place where I would be working. *Working?* I thought I was going to go to school! School was two days a week, four days of actual hands-on work being a goffer, working alongside a master of the trade and generally being his slave. The seventh day was for studies, not rest. The discipline in retrospect was strict but fair; at times, it seemed extreme. I was 14, homesick, surrounded by family and new friends but remained the most lonesome kid on the block. I sorely missed my lost American life.

My uncle's business was building, servicing, and repairing anything diesel, primarily huge diesel trucks. It soon became apparent I had little talent and even less enthusiasm for such work. In fact, I hated it. I am about as handy as a sack full of doorknobs when it comes to anything mechanical.

My inability coupled with my unhappiness soon became evident. I continually asked to be returned to the States. I was told that I was doing just fine and would soon be given work of my own to complete with a new lad as *my* slave. Instead of happily accepting this news, it scared the hell out of me. I knew I wasn't ready.

My academic grades during this period were acceptable, but my work on the trucks or machines was not. My work often had to be redone by a more proficient mechanic. As time passed, I grew increasingly homesick. One day, two Russian MIG fighters flew overhead so fast they flew ahead of their sound: They were supersonic. The resulting sonic boom broke windows, scaring the life out of everyone. These flights were common. I looked forward each day to their low passes. Something about them excited me. Several years would pass before I would again experience and appreciate those feelings for what they were.

When my mother discovered that illegal Russian or Eastern bloc overflights were daily harassing Bavaria, I was on my way home via a TWA Super Constellation. Thank God!

2

THE MID YEARS!

Returning from Germany, I was enrolled in St. Francis DeSales High, a Catholic high school in Lockport, NY. The Jesuit priests were rough, often obtaining your full attention with a quick smack behind your head. It was nothing like today's public-school system. Corporal punishment in any form is now forbidden. In those days, most parents of Catholic school children approved of and encouraged the disciplinary measures employed by the nuns and priests.

My school grades were good, but my home life with my stepdad continued to worsen. I was a little out of control and fed up with school, but I hung in there.

Frequent arguments with my stepdad and badgering by my mom and older brother to take an interest in something were hard to handle. Everyone meant well, but I had no idea what I wanted to do with my life, and at that point had no interest in finding out what it might be. I just wanted a normal teenage life. I felt that I had missed much of my youth with the German experience.

I deeply resented being sent out of the country for practically two years. I found myself out of touch with the latest American movies and music. I didn't know who Elvis Presley was until weeks after my return. I resented my stepdad's drinking which always ended in arguments between Mom, me, and him.

Mom was always crying it seemed. This really tore at me. Graduation day from high school was enlistment day in the U.S. Navy.

My older brother was in chiropractic school with an assured future ahead. I had to find my own way. The Navy seemed a good idea.

Entering the Navy, one had to sit for a battery of aptitude tests. All my tests indicated an aptitude for anything electronic. I felt comfortable with that. Turned out that what I was comfortable with and what the Navy needed where two different things. I was assigned as a machinist mate. Are you kidding me?

It had to be a mistake; it wasn't! A machinist mate had little to do with machines such as metal lathes but rather the rating covered everything from the handling of industrial gases to the repair and maintenance of the ships' washing machines, refrigeration and the distilling of fresh water from seawater in the salt water evaporators. I spent my entire enlistment, for the most part, below ships decks.

While serving aboard ship, I was introduced to the United States Armed Forces Institute (USAFI). It offered all types of classes. I took several. They were a wonderful resource throughout my enlistment.

All during my entire four years active and two-year active reserve enlistment, I constantly asked to be reassigned, to change my rate as it was called, all to no avail. The machinist mate rating was categorized as "critical" and could not be changed. I was screwed!

I was aboard ship for almost my entire enlistment, serving aboard a fast-moving destroyer and a more benign destroyer tender. I was only seasick once: on my first cruise. It was never a problem again. When my four-year enlistment was ending, I was asked to "ship-over," i.e., re-enlist.

I thought about it for some time, asking once again to be reassigned to a new rating. Once again refused. That refusal led to my future as a civilian.

I loved the Navy, loved the ships, but clearly, it was time to leave.

I was discharged from the Navy at Mayport Naval Base in Florida. I had been married six months before my discharge. Marriage was a life-changing event. Trying to decide where we should call home was both exciting and scary. I was instantly faced with zero prospects of making a decent living with no means of providing for a wife. I became painfully aware of my lack of skills. The constant fear in my gut tore at me every day.

We eventually settled on Newport, Rhode Island. During my early years in the Navy, I had been based in Newport and really liked it. I had an ulterior motive.

Flying Vagabond

3

SHOWBIZ, HERE I COME, OR SO I THOUGHT!

E arly in my Navy sojourn, I had met a man while hitchhiking back to Newport from visiting my folks in upstate NY. He was, as it turned out, a former singer and actor, having performed in several Broadway shows. He took a liking to me and treated me to several weekend trips to New York City. There, I met several producers and directors and through them eventually was cast in a few professional plays as an extra or as part of a chorus singing my heart out in *Oklahoma* at the Warwick Rhode Island theater in the round. Rehearsals were five or six hours long before curtain and were primarily for me to get the *blocking* (stage placement) down and hopefully to develop a stage presence. Being hardly noticed, I had fun. I had no union credentials. The producer was a good friend of my mentor and considered it a trial period to check me out. No one ever asked for my union card, and if they had, I was to refer them to the producer. You simply could not get away with anything approaching this today—all of this between Naval cruises. I always seemed to get a 72 hour or 48-hour pass while in port when I needed it. I didn't make every performance but was having the time of my life.

Introduced to singing and acting coaches, I was told that I had some latent talent and with proper guidance and culturing, was worth nurturing. Although nervous about all the attention, I began fantasizing about a showbiz career, post-Navy

I was being pampered by these people. God knows why, but I loved it! It was understood that when I was discharged from the service, I would return to Newport or New York and hopefully realize that fantasized career in showbiz. However, I wasn't supposed to get married, and that is exactly what I had done...STUPIDO! My acting career went south instantly once they discovered I was married. No one in show business seemed interested in me anymore. I really didn't understand it, but that's how it was.

I was told that a show business career would involve a lot of coast to coast travel and that my hitchhiking friend John was to be my agent. Agent for what? Somehow, my getting married did not fit into John's plans. It became apparent that John envisioned a career not only for me but for himself. Personally, I never thought I had a great deal of talent for show business. On the other hand, John assured me that you didn't need much talent to become an actor.

Years later, I became the pilot of a movie producer, discovering firsthand how true John's statements were regarding actors. Many were great, many had no talent. They got by on their good looks and publicity, and a few are very famous today. Being a movie producer's pilot, I was granted access to many major movie studios. Watching some well-known stars struggle through take after take of a scene was enlightening. Quite often, children of established movie idols, making their acting debut, were shouted encouragement from off-camera by well-meaning parents.

I quickly learned that if you do something often enough, you will eventually get it right. More than a few *stars* were literally thrown into acting, as that was the family business.

In later years, flying mostly international trips, I had an opportunity to audition for a local community playhouse production called *"Greetings"* at St. Augustine, Florida's Limelight Theater. To my surprise, I was awarded the lead role. Several plays followed including a very minor non-speaking role in the movie *"Recount"* starring Kevin Spacey.

Acting was fun, but it failed to produce the income we needed to support a family.

Flying Vagabond

4

MAKING A LIVING

Returning to Newport, Rhode Island, I found work at a place called The Newport Creamery as an assistant manager. The creamery was known throughout New England for its delicious ice cream. It was also a luncheonette. My parents had owned a few restaurants where I worked gaining restaurant experience. I had done everything from washing dishes and waiting tables to short order cooking. I was up to the challenge.

One of the creamery customers was a district manager of World Book encyclopedias. One day, striking up a conversation, he asked me if I wanted to make some extra cash as a door to door encyclopedia salesman.

This was long before the internet. Encyclopedias where *the* source material especially for school children. I decided to give it a shot on a part-time basis and found that I was good at it, outselling the top performer in his district two to one. I was awarded a bag full of fifty silver dollars with dates as early as 1880 as a prize. I spent them! I wonder what they would be worth today? That was not the first of many lessons.

The bubble of my success soon burst when my wife was summoned to Ohio, (her home state) by her mother to help care for her ailing grandmother.

I didn't want to leave Newport but had very little to say in the matter. Looking back, this turned out to be a very fortuitous move.

5

WHAT ARE ALL THOSE SWITCHES?

I found a job at the Cleveland airport. Hired as a service supervisor by a company called Sky Chefs, it was my job to see to the catering of several airlines. I also moonlighted at Dobb's House Catering, another airline caterer, working as supervisor three nights a week. That's when airlines fed passengers with quality food on most flights, which only happens now on international flights.

One day while supervising the loading of the galley of a brand-new Northwest Airlines Boeing 727, I struck up a conversation with the copilot of the aircraft. Giving me a tour of the cockpit, I was impressed with all the switches and lights. Pointing out the specific function of each as he spoke left me dazzled and excited.

After a few minutes of staring at the array of lights and switches, a voice behind us said, "Excuse me." It was the captain.

I had a hundred questions for the two pilots. I suddenly felt that same feeling I had when those MIG fighters flew over me in Germany.

After doing their best to answer my questions, the captain spoke up saying: "If you have that kind of interest, why don't you take a lesson or two and see if this life might be for you?" That's exactly what I did!

Flying Vagabond

6

HOW MUCH MONEY DOES IT TAKE TO FLY? WHY ALL OF IT OF COURSE!

One day soon after, while driving home, I noticed the Strongsville Ohio airport. How strange that I never noticed it before; I passed it every day. There was a sign out front that advertised an *"Introductory Free Airplane Ride."* I turned in.

Immediately introduced to a very young flight instructor, I mentioned the sign for a free introductory flight. While walking me out to a small aircraft, he extolled the virtues of flying. Reaching the aircraft, a Piper Colt (PA-20), he introduced me to the *walk-around inspection* that every pilot does before every flight. Completing the walk-around, we boarded the aircraft, started the engine, and taxied toward the runway. An engine run-up just before turning onto the runway made certain the engine was working as it should. After that, we commenced the takeoff roll. Climbing to 10,000 feet, I was thrilled with the fact that I was flying, well, at least riding. Climbing took quite a while as the Piper Colt didn't have a lot of power—108 HP. The instructor said we were climbing to 10,000 feet to allow me a breathtaking view of our surroundings. What he really wanted to do was scare the hell out of me.

Once at 10,000 feet, he closed the throttle, pushed hard on one of the rudder pedals and pulled back on the control column, allowing the aircraft to enter a full-blown spiraling stall. An aircraft stalls when it no longer can sustain level flight generally due to a loss of airspeed resulting in a loss of lift.

As the nose dropped, the aircraft commenced a spin to the left leaving us hanging from our seatbelts, with a wide-eyed view of terra firma. I am not sure when we recovered from the spin, but I loved it and asked if we could do it again. Mister smarty pants was very surprised at my reaction and simply said, "You'll do."

I was hooked. Signing up for lessons, buying every textbook, plotter, chart and an E6B (a hand-held aviation slide rule) I was on my way!

I flew almost daily, accumulating some 20 hours of instruction. Soon, my flight instructor was hired by Mohawk Airlines as a first officer. Assigned a new instructor, I quickly progressed.

Asked to contact UNICOM (a common aviation frequency used at non-tower operated airports) by my new instructor, I was at a loss. He seemed stunned that I did not know what UNICOM was. It seems my first instructor was just burning up my money, putting his time in while he sought an airline job. I discovered I should have soloed several hours earlier. Feeling cheated, I decided to go somewhere more professional to acquire my licenses.

Reading everything I could about aviation and discovering that the commercial airlines were on a hiring spree, I decided that I would quit my great-paying job at Sky Chefs, get a loan and attend a dedicated flying school full time.

Hopkins Airport had a semi-formal dining room also operated by Sky Chefs. I was often called upon to host arriving guests along with two of the hostesses. On my last day at Sky Chef where I shared hosting duties with two ladies, one of them asked if I could provide her a ride home. She explained she had taken a taxi to work, as her automobile hadn't started that morning.

"Of course, I would be happy to!" I said.

Arriving at her home and invited in for a farewell drink, we spent close to an hour reminiscing my tenure at Sky Chef. After a goodbye hug and well wishes, I left for home.

My hosting duties required me to wear a white sports jacket with black tuxedo trousers. Later, while driving home, I noticed my sports jacket had the unmistakable and tell-tale fragrance of "Eau de Parfum." I had been hugged by several of the hostesses wishing me well transferring wonderful fragrances to my sports jacket. Fearful that the wrong conclusion might be reached when I arrived home igniting past suspicions of infidelity, I removed the jacket. While driving, I placed my finger through the small loop at the base of the collar and held it out of the window in the hope of *airing* it out. For several miles, things went well, that is, until the small fabric loop I had my finger through, broke. The jacket flew onto the highway and was promptly run over by the car to my rear. Stopping immediately and waiting for traffic to pass, I retrieved the jacket. Thankfully, a close inspection revealed no visible signs of the unfortunate mishap, or so I thought, as it was very dark. Arriving home, I found my wife asleep on the sofa, waking as I entered. After a quick brush kiss, I walked toward the bedroom when I was brought up short.

"Whoa, whoa! Come back here! Turn around!" she said.

"What?" I said.

"Did you get run over on your way home?" she asked while brushing the back of my jacket.

"What are you talking about?"

"Take off your jacket!" she demanded.

Now what? I wondered. There on the back of the jacket was a very distinct set of tire marks running straight up the center of the jacket.

"How do you explain those tire tracks?"

My Momma always told me to tell the truth, so I did.

She wasn't having any of it and accused me of all sorts of nefarious behavior behind her back. So much for the truth. Sometimes, damned if you do, damned if you don't!

The sofa took some getting used to!

I settled on Santa Barbara California's University of the Air located in the small community of Goleta, California, an adjacent community to Santa Barbara. I applied and was accepted with a planned start date two weeks hence. Basically terrified, anxious, and unsure of myself, I started my instruction.

In just over three months of daily flight instruction, with weekly flight checks to observe my progress, I was recommended for an FAA private pilot's flight check. Successfully passing that, I was quickly recommended for a commercial pilot's license flight check followed a week later by an FAA instrument flight check. After some additional training, I passed an FAA multi-engine flight check in a light twin aircraft. Whew! I had successfully passed all of them and was over the moon. The ink was barely dry on my newly-acquired certificates when I started typing up resumes. Look out airlines, here I come!

7

RUDE AWAKENING!

I discovered that with no college credits beyond flight school and with very little flight time, the prospect of an airline job was almost nonexistent. With debt mounting daily and my wife becoming increasingly concerned, my blood pressure was climbing. A rude awakening indeed!

Deciding to return to Cleveland and Cleveland Hopkins Airport, I attempted to get my old job back only to find it was no longer available. While seated dejectedly at the airport coffee shop and feeling lost, the station manager for Northwest Airlines took the seat next to me. He recognized me from my airline catering days. After catching up on my absence and hearing I needed a job, he offered to hire and train me as an agent for Northwest. His name was John La Montagne. I shall never forget his kindness.

Mr. La Montagne tried to get me hired with Northwest as a pilot but to no avail. The old, 'you don't have enough flight time' ergo experience, kept coming up, not to mention my minimal educational background.

As an employee of Northwest Airlines, I was given airline pass privileges, and Mr. La Montagne encouraged me to use them as often as I needed in pursuit of my dream.

One day, I noticed a large *taildragger* (tail wheel) aircraft on approach to Cleveland airport and became fascinated as it bounced several times on landing. I had just finished my shift at Northwest and watched as it taxied to a series of aircraft hangars near where my car was parked. Driving over after my shift, I introduced myself to the crew. They were from Zantop International Airlines of Detroit, MI. After mentioning that I was a new commercial pilot looking for employment, they suggested that I apply ASAP, as the airline was currently hiring. I wasted little time in applying!

8

ALL I WANT IS AN INTERVIEW! I'LL TAKE IT FROM THERE!

After applying with Zantop at the home office in Detroit, I waited and waited but never heard a word. Northwest flew daily to Detroit from Cleveland. Detroit was the home office of Zantop. I used my Northwest passes to visit Detroit airport as often as I could, but after three months, I became frustrated.

I desperately wanted an interview. Zantop personnel said I should be patient. After a half-dozen trips to Detroit, I was plumb out of patience. One day, frustrated, I took it upon myself to find the chief pilot's office. Security was rather lax in those days. I walked through the halls and walkways of the old hangar until I came upon an office marked, Captain John Palmer, CHIEF PILOT!

Sheepishly opening the door, I entered an anti-office with another door marked PRIVATE to my left. A woman looked up from her typing and asked: "Can I help you?"

To which I replied, "Err, ahhh well, I was hoping to talk to Captain Palmer."

"Regarding?" she said.

"An interview for a job as a pilot," I managed to say, feeling as though I may have bitten off more than I could possibly chew.

With a rather disdainful look, I was told that Captain Palmer did not grant pre-hire interviews; personnel did. She asked who directed me to his office. I explained I simply found his office without direction, explaining I had already been through the personnel drill to no avail.

She said, "I am sorry. That is the course every new hire must take."

Not being one of those yet, and with my resume and application in hand and noticing the adjacent door, I asked if that was the entrance to Captain Palmer's office. Answering in the affirmative, I steeled my resolve and rushed the door marked PRIVATE with the secretary in hot pursuit screaming at me to stop. My newly discovered resolve was nearly defeated when to my horror there were two doors to this office, which were separated by only one or two feet—a safety device builders once employed to help slow the spread of fire.

My momentum sent me crashing into the second door, announcing my arrival. Considerably deflated, I sheepishly pushed open the second door and found I had positioned myself in the middle of a meeting. The director of operations, chief pilot, and chief engineer of the airline sat staring in shocked silence.

The man I assumed to be the chief pilot finally spoke,

"Who the fuck *are you* and what the fuck do *you want*?"

Pushing past, grabbing and pulling me by the arm, the secretary attempted to explain that she tried to stop me.

Ignoring her while waving her off, the voice once again said louder; "Who the fuck *ARE* you and what the fuck *DO* you want?"

Nearly blinded by fear, with a loud pounding in my ears, I addressed the voice in a barely audible response saying I had spent the last three months seeking an interview, to no avail.

The application that I had been waving frantically was snatched from my hand.

After perusing it, a quizzical look accompanied by a slight smile crossed the face of the one who I assumed was Captain Palmer.

"You want a job as *WHAT?*" he asked.

"A pilot!" I said.

Returning to my application, he asked one of the other men seated at the table.

"What the fuck is a Cherokee?"

"An Indian," the other two said.

This was listed as one of the aircraft that I had flown—a small single-engine Piper aircraft.

"And an Apache and a Comanche?" he asked.

More Indians, the other two responded. They were similar small Piper aircraft.

My resolve beginning to ebb, I stuttered that everyone had to start somewhere, flying something and that that was my background so far.

Mustering courage, I brashly asked for an opportunity to begin my flying career and added I had chosen their airline as that vehicle.

"Son, my wife's legs have more time in the air than you do!" he said.

Captain Palmer sat silently staring at me for what seemed at least five minutes but was probably nearer five seconds. Looking out of the window, pointing to a large tail dragger aircraft, the same type I had seen landing and bouncing at Cleveland, he said:

"Do you think you can fly one of those?"

Not exactly sure what *one of those* was, in a very small voice I responded,

"Yes, I do."

Smiling while placing my application on his desk, he said:

"We have a C-46 class starting next Wednesday, October 10 at YIP-Willow Run Airport—hangar number one, 0800. Be there!

You're a ballsy little fucker and deserve a chance, now get the hell outta my office."

Walking out to the ramp, I stood under the nose of this almost three-story tall behemoth called a C-46, wondering what I had gotten myself into.

9

DETERMINED!

Studying my butt off, I did well in ground school, flight training was a different story. You learned only one way— by flying the actual aircraft. First, one had to pass an instrument flight check conducted in a link trainer—a small box with a cover that closed placed on a pedestal simulating a generic aircraft cockpit with rudimentary aircraft instrumentation. This *box*, when energized, produced motion in one axis only: lateral. I passed!

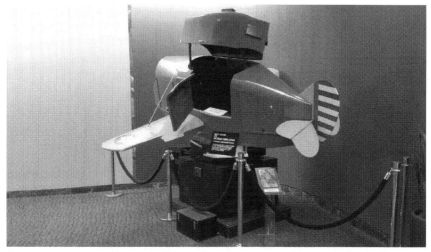

The link trainer.

Note the basic instrumentation.

Captain Jack Webber had been assigned as my training captain and instructor. I thank God to this day for Jack Weber's patience and understanding.

As a new hire, I was allotted a maximum of 10 hours of instruction. If you didn't cut it, you were gone. I had one problem after another. Nothing was easy. The 10 hours came and went when Captain Jack pulled me aside in a vacant classroom. Explaining I had reached my allotment of training time, I became terrified I was about to be washed out when he said:

"I have an idea, but when I tell you, it must remain confidential."

I thought, who would I tell?

Listening intently, he mentioned that he had already spoken to another captain who agreed to give me a few extra hours of flight training, as he thought I was worth trying to salvage.

The problem was, the training would have to be at night, and it would have to be done under the guise of maintenance flights and was to be with Captain Bill Stone. My hopes soared!

10

LADY, YOU WANT TO KNOW IF THIS OLD AIRPLANE IS SAFE TO FLY? JUST HOW IN THE WORLD DO YOU THINK IT GOT TO BE THIS OLD?

—Jim Tavenner

Even though I was new, I had heard about Captain William (Bill) Stone. *Wild Bill*, as he was known by several new-hire student pilots, enjoyed a reputation that struck fear into the hearts of all new hires. He reportedly ate copilots for lunch. Frankly, I was terrified. To be instructed by him and at night seemed close too impossible. My night flying experience was extremely limited.

Captain Jack told me that Bill Stone was one of the best despite his reputation. He was sure that Bill's no-nonsense instruction, would quickly—*illuminate*—my difficulties, *gently* point out my shortcomings, while *patiently* demonstrating proper technique. All this would occur while Captain Bill Stone carefully observed my desperate attempts to tame the hardest, most challenging airplane I had ever flown. There is an old cliché that says the definition of a complex airplane is: landing a taildragger with a 20-knot quartering crosswind. I was about to lend credence to that adage.

Attempting to introduce myself at our first meeting and ignoring my outstretched hand, he said: "You can call me by my first name: CAPTAIN!"

Training with the "CAPTAIN" started that very night.

Approaching the aircraft, I was asked what I saw as I approached.

Zantop N611Z—a C-46 Curtis Commando, the very aircraft used for my nighttime instruction from the captain.

A view of the office.

This was different! Not sure what to answer, I mumbled something and was immediately told what to look for; chocks (wooden blocks placed under the wheels to keep the aircraft in place) control locks (devices that physically prevented the aircraft controls from moving in the wind) in proximity of equipment around the aircraft, all while pointing out that we should always check for two engines and two wings. There was a reason for that remark. Let me explain.

One of the owners of the airline, Dwayne Zantop, while *in his cups* (i.e., drunk) one dark night, found a lone C-46 on the ramp and approaching from the left side of the aircraft he looked inside. Finding it empty, he bellowed loudly, demanding the aircraft be loaded immediately, all the while casting aspersions on everyone's ancestry. The aircraft hangar was filled with cargo to be shipped, and this was the only aircraft on the ramp.

"But Dwayne!" the loading supervisor pleaded.

Shutting him down immediately, Dwayne started a rant heard across the ramp and through the thick walls of the hangar. Heads poked out of every hangar door. Several attempts to explain why the aircraft was not loaded were ignored.

Demanding a crew be alerted, he screamed for the loaders to get a load together ASAP. "Load the God damn airplane," he bellowed. With wry smiles and shrugged shoulders, a freight load was assembled and loaded aboard. The wry smiles soon gave way to laughter as the flight crew, approaching from the left side of the aircraft, climbed aboard.

Assuming maintenance had completed the walk-around inspection, the copilot pulled the boarding ladder on board after the captain climbed aboard, closed the large freight loading doors, and settled into the cockpit.

The checklist was read to the start engines line. The captain called: "Gimme 12!" This procedure called for the captain to engage the starter thus turning the blades of the starboard or right-side propeller at least 12 times to mitigate a hydraulic lock.

When the copilot looked out of his window toward the engine to commence a blade count, he turned to the captain; struggling to maintain a straight face, he said:

"Twelve what?"

"Twelve blades damn it!" the already disgruntled captain said.

The copilot snickered while the captain, looking quite puzzled, said: "What?"

The copilot, attempting to contain himself, could only get out a "No…"

The captain, now fully aware that he was about to hear something pretty ridiculous, said, "Let me guess. No engine!"

The copilot, now laughing hysterically, blurted out:

"No wing!"

It seems that the wing had been removed because of a previous ground collision accident. Not only was that embarrassing; in time it became a legend among *freight dogs*[2] everywhere.

I quickly learned that if *you* are flying crew, do your own walk-around inspection! It's a great story, more so because it's true.

---

[2] Freight dog: a term of endearment used among cargo pilots to describe their piloting of freight status.

Flying Vagabond

11

A WILD RIDE WITH WILD BILL

Wild Bill continued the walk-around administering me an oral examination of the aircraft, pointing out things that I would never have thought to look at.

His usual manner of speaking was gruff, rough and no-nonsense. I was clearly terrified of him and dreaded what was in store.

After the walk-around inspection of the aircraft and while seated in the cockpit he provided a detailed explanation, of everything from the aircraft systems to instrument flying procedures.

This guy was tough, and we hadn't even started engines yet. We, that is, I managed to start the engines with only a modest amount of backfiring and belching of the temperamental Wright Cyclone R-2800 engines.

Captain Bill taxied out, putting us in position on the runway. He called for the tail wheel to be locked. This was very important as an assist in keeping the aircraft tracking straight during the takeoff roll. Calling for and receiving takeoff clearance, Captain Bill wiggled the control yoke—*ailerons*—indicating it was my aircraft and throttles. I advanced the throttles slowly. The aircraft accelerated rapidly, reaching takeoff speed quickly. Lifting off, I gave the signal to raise the landing gear.

Hand signals were the order of the day, as the engine roar made it impossible to hear. This required letting go of the throttles with my left hand. Suddenly, Wild Bill reduced power on the number one (left) engine simulating an engine failure on takeoff. Every pilot's worse nightmare and the worst possible time to experience such an event.

I gave the signal for flaps up, adjusting aircraft trim. The aircraft was simply a bear to control with one engine inoperative. Maintaining control required that full opposite rudder be applied to compensate for the torque of the opposite operating engine, my leg shaking in the effort.

At the same time, it took both hands to keep the wings level. There were no hydraulically-boosted controls on these old airplanes. The throttle, vibrating from the torque of the remaining engine, started vibrating toward idle power. This further reduced power decreasing what was already a minimal climb of about 100 feet per minute.

Wild Bill was ready. Advancing the number two (right) throttle back up to takeoff power, he reached across the cockpit, grabbed my left hand in a vice grip and placed it on the working engine throttle, as I had been using both hands to control the aircraft.

My right leg was extended fully on the rudder shaking violently. My right arm ached holding the right aileron to also help counter the torque. The fingers of my left hand were going numb due to the death grip of holding the throttle forward.

Managing a glance over at Wild Bill, he was watching me very carefully, nodding his head positively while sadistically grinning. *Bastard!*

After reaching 1000 feet, he advanced power on the idling engine, setting the power to a climb setting, never saying a word. Hell, an attaboy would have been nice! Already a physical wreck as we had only been airborne a few minutes, I dreaded what I feared was to come.

Under Bill's watchful eye, several ILS (instrument landing system) approaches, several missed approaches, a balked landing with both engines operating, several with a simulated engine failure were introduced. These were followed by three or four NDB (non-directional) approaches, an outdated non-precision approach, with few still in service today.

We made three VOR approaches. The VOR station transmitted a signal in 360 degrees and was always the center of the circle. The direction you approached the station would determine your bearing from or to that station.

This was an old freighter with stiff controls—no power assist. You needed to lift weights regularly to manhandle this aircraft, I felt like a tightrope walker on a soaped line in a rainstorm.

After two nights of Captain Bill yelling, cussing, screaming at me above the roar of the engines, I was finally given his blessing and was put forward for the F/O (first officer) check ride.

Flying Vagabond

12

END OF TRAINING:
THE DREADED CHECK RIDE

Captain Ernie Fife conducted my check ride in the C-46. Ernie's reputation preceded him. He was tough. Of course, at this stage, every examiner scared the hell out of me. Most were cross-trained on DC-6s and 7s with some of them flying the Argosy AW-650, a large four-engine, twin-boomed freighter, the L-188 Lockheed Electra and the newly-acquired DC-8s. Every one of them had thousands of hours of experience. Clearly, I was intimidated.

The check ride over, I was left to secure the aircraft and in the dark as to the outcome. Told to meet Captain Ernie in one of the classrooms above the hangar floor, I hurried to learn my fate, fearful that these past few weeks were wasted effort.

Entering the classroom, Captain Ernie extended his hand. He said, "Congratulations, first officer," as he handed me my wings. Happy and relieved simply could not describe my emotional state. My flying career, my dream, was beginning at last!

Flying Vagabond

13

DUMBO

The venerable C-46 painted in the ATC (Air Transport Command) colors. This aircraft flew thousands of missions flying over "The Hump" the Himalaya Mountains. The C-46 Commando was the largest twin-engine aircraft having the largest fuselage flown during WWII. There were 3,181 built.[3] (Air Force Museum, Fairborn, Ohio.)

---

[3] *Specifications:* Span: 108 ft. 0 in. (32.9 m) Length:76 ft. 4 in. (23.3 m), Height: 22 ft. 0 in. (6.7 m), Weight: 51,000 lbs. (23,154 kg.) Engines: Two Pratt &Whitney R-2800s of 2000 hp each.
Performance: Maximum Speed: 245 mph (394 km/hr.) Cruising Speed: 175 mph (282 km/hr.) Range: 1,200 miles 1931 km.) Service Ceiling: 27,600 ft. (8,418 m.)

The C-46, affectionately referred to as Dumbo, was a pure bitch to fly. My affection for the aircraft was a long time coming. My first trip captain in Dumbo, with me as a brand-new first officer, was with Captain Palmer, the same Captain Palmer whose meeting I had interrupted so long ago. He knew that I had made it through training and couldn't wait to see how the *ballsy little fucker* was doing. I was never as nervous or more frightened of anything in my life than I was on that trip. I made a few dumb mistakes. He smiled at some of my stumbles, easing my anxiety. The trip was a round robin YIP/MKC/YIP (Detroit/Kansas City /Detroit.) Returning to YIP, he left the aircraft with barely a word, but I think he had a grin on his face!

Struggling to become proficient, I looked forward to flying from the right seat whenever given the opportunity. The airline employed some 600 pilots, most of whom were former military C-46 pilots. These *retreads* provided a fertile field of experience.

I am convinced that *bouncing it on* time after time, recovering each time from an imminent crash barely seconds away, leaving me flush with adrenaline, served as a wonderful learning experience. However, it did little in overcoming my anxiety and intimidation by these more experienced aviators.

Often, after demonstrating my lack of prowess with the machine, I was frequently told, "Sit there and don't touch nuthin' till I tell ya," by some of them. This only increased my anxiety. Nonetheless, I tried to display a fair amount of self-confidence. It was all a façade.

Discovering that I would be flying with captains who had thousands of hours, most of which had been garnered while flying under the most extreme conditions of WWII, made me more than a bit nervous. Many of them, while revered for their wartime experiences, were also very human. Some were egomaniacs, who had little use for us "snot-nosed newbies."

14

FORGED IN THE CRUCIBLE OF WAR!

Most of these C-46 captains had flown the "Hump" during WWII. The *Hump* was a name given by Allied pilots during WWII to the eastern end of the Himalayan Mountains.

Flying military transport aircraft such as the C-46, Curtis-Wright Commando, and C-47 (the Douglas DC-3 as it is known in its civilian life) from India to China resupplying the Chinese war effort of Chiang Kai-shek. This was officially known as the Air Transport Command (ATC) originally being referred to as the *India-China Ferry Command.*

Flying over the Himalayas was extremely dangerous at best, made much more difficult by a lack of reliable charts, and an almost total absence of radio navigation aids, along with poor, if any, information about the weather.

For its efforts during its 42-month history, and after a great cost in men and equipment, the ATC was awarded the *Presidential Unit Citation* in January 1942 by Franklin D. Roosevelt.

This was the first such award made to a non-combat organization. Here I was, sitting next to some of those same guys.

These captains were tough, brave beyond words; heroes to a man. I endured punishment from more than a few of these *Rough Riders* over time.

Some were ego-driven rogue pilots who had forgotten their early struggles making the same mistakes we younger and inexperienced pilots were making. No doubt they had learned from a few rogue pilots in *their* past, being equally mistreated. A few were still dealing with demons of past experiences, seeking comfort from alcohol. Others; well adjusted, considerate, and kind; provided moments that were humbling, gratifying, and wonderfully enlightening. Some were great mentors.

My favorite was Captain Bud.

15

THE GOOD

I have flown with many pilots in my 40+ year career; a few stand out in my memory.

The glint of some of these rogue pilots' halos was beginning to tarnish. Things changed when I was assigned a trip with Captain Bud![4]

Captain Bud took me under his wing, gently and professionally guiding, advising, and instructing. He allowed me to fly the *beast* (his name for Dumbo) from the left seat for the first time. This was a high honor, also potentially dangerous.

Captain Bud's instruction, his infinite patience, understanding and willingness to allow me to experience the thrill, nay, the work required of getting the *beast* to the right place at the right time from the left seat (the captain's seat) with the least amount of effort remains a cherished memory.

Captain Bud let me discover the wrong way several times before discovering the right way to handle ole Dumbo. He was a consummate professional in every sense of the word.

I often harken back to Bud's mantra of, "self-discovery is a wonderful thing" as I now instruct and teach today's younger and yet uninitiated airmen. Thanks, bud!

---

[4] Things have changed considerably since the 1960s. No one would dare lay hands on you today. However, then—no HR!

Captain Bud's instruction and guidance prepared me to eventually check out as captain of a C-46 a few years later. I know he would have been proud. I was saddened to hear of Bud's passing while flying for Air America during the Vietnam War.

Bud left our cargo airline in 1969, wanting me to go with him. Being a Navy vet and having served my time, now with a family, the last thing that I wanted to do was to put myself in harm's way once again despite the great pay.

Bud was shot down and killed while orbiting over a firebase while it was under attack, dropping well-needed supplies to the besieged troops.

Bud's earnings were substantial for that day and time. He had purchased a farm in Ohio prior to his last deployment. He sent me the address that if I was ever in the neighborhood and he was home, I should drop by.

A few years later, while flying for the U.S. Air Force Logistics Air Command based at Wright-Patterson Air Force Base, I passed Captain Bud's farm almost daily on the way to the base saying a little prayer for him as I passed.

Air America, Phan Thiet-Vietnam

16

THE BAD: CAPTAIN PETE!

As a new reserve copilot on the C-46, dispatch called me to report to operations ASAP! When I asked for more info; "Just get here ASAP" came the reply. They were always in crisis it seemed.

"You will be filled in when you get here!"

Arriving as quickly as I could, I was handed a confirmed ticket on Eastern Airlines to Atlanta, GA.[5]

"Rent a car; drive to the Macon, GA airport; locate a C-46, tail number 616ZA." Told it would be on the maintenance ramp at the airline's outlying heavy maintenance facility, I was to locate the captain who would probably be asleep and waiting for me in the cockpit.

It was about 0200 the following morning when I finally arrived at Macon airport, located the aircraft, and discovered Captain Pete asleep as advertised, scrunched in the left seat, feet resting on the throttle quadrant, an empty pint bottle of Four Roses whiskey resting on his chest. The cockpit reeking of cheap booze.

I was still new to the airline, inexperienced and at a loss as to what should happen next. Trying to rouse the captain proved futile.

---

[5] Zantop International had reciprocal agreements to allow crew members from different airlines to fly space available on their flights. The urgency of getting the aircraft back to Detroit ASAP, required a full fare ticket purchase.

Observing lights coming from open hangar doors, I searched for a phone inside to call dispatch. There were no cell phones in those days. Not wanting to call, I didn't really know what else to do.

The company had previously told me they needed this aircraft back to base in Detroit ASAP. It appeared to me that would be a day or so away, if at all with this captain.

Relieved to see another of our company first officers pre-flighting a different C-46, I approached him with my dilemma. Knowing he had been with the airline several years longer than I had, I hoped perhaps he could offer me advice and/or help. He had recently been captain qualified and often used as a reserve captain when the needs of the airline required it. Mentioning my dilemma, he came up with what I thought was a genius plan: he would fly my assigned aircraft back from the left seat *single pilot*. A difficult proposition to say the least; pour Captain Pete into the right seat, strap him in and see to it he got to his car back at home base to sleep it off. He would leave Pete's car keys with one of the ramp personnel.

I was to replace him as first officer on his aircraft, which was also destined for Detroit. This was put forward to his captain, a friend of Captain Pete's. He was skeptical but finally agreed to the plan.

Both trips were uneventful, arriving safely in Detroit just before dawn. Dispatch was kept out of the loop regarding the swap. I was sworn to secrecy. Paperwork was completed as usual with no changes, and no one the wiser...or so we thought!

As it turned out, security had observed Captain Pete being helped to his car by his first officer.

Noticing the captain seemed to be staggering, the security guard's suspicions were aroused. He decided to keep a watchful eye on the car.

With the approach of daylight, the security guard, deciding to take a closer look, discovered Pete slumped in the front seat, appearing unconscious and drooling. Trying the door and finding it locked, and thinking Pete was either dead or dying, he broke out the driver's side window to revive poor old Pete and get him some help.

Awakening with a start from his drunken slumber, Pete smashed his fist into the security guard's nose, turning it into a bloody mess.

Observing the commotion, the *ramp rat* (men who guided and marshaled aircraft on the ramp) who had been entrusted with Captain Pete's car keys, came running. He had been recruited earlier by Captain Pete's savior copilot and was instructed to keep an eye on him. Arriving on scene, he saw a heavily-bleeding security guard and a wide-awake Captain Pete. Offered his keys, Pete quickly realized that they had been taken from him for safekeeping. He ripped them from the extended hand, started the car and drove off weaving his way toward the airport exit. All of this was observed by an arriving flight crew who promptly reported this to operations.

Called to give my version of events and being a newbie, I was severely chastised for not notifying airline dispatch when I discovered Captain Pete in his cups. I got off with a warning. All other offending participants were relieved of flying duties without pay for 30 days.

The security guard was awarded a certificate for his diligence and given two weeks off with pay to nurse that terribly smashed nose. The airline eventually fired Captain Pete.

I was told much later that he had died in a terrible auto accident. No one knew if he had been drunk or not, but if I were a betting man...!

Flying Vagabond

17

THE UGLY: CAPTAIN GEORGE!

Then there was Captain George! One of the original WWII Hump pilots. Damn, I learned a lot from him, just not as much as from Captain Bud!

He was a hell of a C-46 pilot but completely unskilled in social graces. Assigned to fly with Captain George for the first time, I couldn't wait! I had heard his handling of the C-46 was almost God-like.

Approaching from across the room, I noticed Captain George was wearing a scarf. Having been told by more seasoned copilots that George always wore a scarf loosely about his neck in all seasons, I had also been warned: "Don't ever touch his scarf."

When I asked why, I was told with a wry smile that I would find out soon enough. Until then, "Just don't do it," they said.

He introduced himself to me in a matter of fact manner. I cautiously eyed the scarf about his neck. Walking me over to the fueling desk to ensure that I gave the correct fuel order exactly as he specified, and standing next to the re-fueling desk, I noticed George was intermittently wiping his running nose disgustedly on *THE SCARF!*

It immediately became clear why I was told never to touch his scarf. I pretended not to notice, but it became even more distracting when he began to *snort* into it.

To me, his snorting sounded something akin to a wild boar rutting in the wild. The fueling person was busy with several aircraft fueling requests and didn't notice. *He should have!*

The fuel ordering process was taking longer than it should have, when suddenly, Captain George made a sound, reminiscent of a whale blowing air through its blowhole followed by a rather large disgusting yellow/greenish slimy mess being deposited at the fuelers elbow and on his paperwork.

It seems that George had to blow his abundantly full nose, letting fly with one nostril after the other. A look of surprise, disgust, and revulsion came over both of us.

Jumping back from his desk, the young fueler, fire in his eyes, took after George who was rapidly walking toward the exit, no doubt aware of what he had just deposited upon the desk, wiping his nose with the scarf as he went. It took four of us to keep George from being pummeled to death.

After being freed from the grip of the irate fuel guy, Captain George continued to the aircraft, climbed up into the cockpit, and waited for the fuel truck.

Our flight departed on time. Not a word was ever mentioned about the incident until we reached our cruise altitude when I took my career in my hands and dared question, my captain.

I simply said;

"So, captain, that was pretty disgusting back there."

"Yeah, I thought I was gonna miss the desk," he replied with an impish smile. Nuff said!

Another incident with George took place after landing at Atlanta's Hartsfield Airport. While our aircraft was being unloaded, we opted for some lunch across the way at Morrison's Cafeteria well within walking distance. In those days, there were few fences nor security to navigate. A quick walk across a busy street was all that was required.

Deciding he didn't need a crosswalk, George commenced walking diagonally across the bustling intersecting streets against the red stop lights overhead.

In all his airline finery with wings and epilates on display and reaching the center of the road literally stopping traffic because of his jaywalking, he hiked his leg and let go with what can only be described as a *Herculean fart*.

One lady whose car window was open comes to mind. She was best described as disgusted while another fellow gave a rousing, thumbs up to George while honking his horn and driving off.

When George retired from the cargo airline shortly thereafter, he requested and received his very own C-46. The airline was about to retire this particular aircraft and awarded it to Captain George.

I had heard that he had applied for his very own FAA part 121 supplemental certificate but doubt he received it.

The aircraft, however, was his to do with as he pleased. I never did find out what he did with it.

Years later I heard that George had passed away. I hope he used that *impish smile* of his with St. Peter 'cause it sure might've helped him get past those pearly gates—if he kept his *nose clean*.

Flying Vagabond

18

OLE RED SOCKS

Many colorful characters filled my early flying career, not the least of which was a little fellow by the name of Captain Al. I am not very tall, about 5'9", but this guy was only about 5'5" and twice as feisty. He always wore very loud red socks with his regulation uniform. His pant legs, always a couple of inches too short, left no doubt who was approaching. Talk about *high waters*, his trousers stopped several inches above the top of his shoes to allow for keeping them dry in the case of rising water. Man, those red socks sure showed up.

I remember one late-night trip, almost all flights were at night, when the weather was foreboding as hell. A squall line ahead of a fast-moving cold front stretched across the Midwest all the way from North Texas through Indiana and Illinois into Canada.

I mentioned this to Captain Al. He looked at me rather strangely and said, "So?"

So, hell, it was a squall line, I thought. Our old aircraft had no airborne radar and no transponder, a device that sends an assigned signal code to air traffic control to aid in positive radar identification among other things.

"So," he says. Anyway, I had heard about this guy. I was told that he had wooden blocks that he attached to the rudder pedals adding a few inches to the pedals. He claimed he couldn't get his seat close enough to get *full rudder travel* if required. How he got away with it is beyond me but in those days, who was looking?

Sure enough, once seated in the captain's seat, he affixed those blocks to the rudder pedals. Never saying a word, he caught me looking and sheepishly explained it was hard for him to reach the pedals. I wondered how he could apply the brakes, which were on the top of those pedals. I made a mental note to be ready to assist as needed.

I just smiled and started reading the *Before Engines Start Checklist.* Little did I know that I would soon be called upon to *get on the rudders* either with him or for him, as we were soon to encounter some God-awful turbulence somewhere over the state of Indiana.

Our trip had been flight planned through the middle of Indiana and through the middle of the squall line. We had been told there were holes in it by meteorology and dispatch, but without radar, we would hardly be able to find those holes.

The takeoff was uneventful, climbing to our cruising altitude of 6000 feet en route to MKC. Cruise power was set, and Captain Al reached over and tapped the yoke indicating that he wanted me to fly. No autopilot in these old birds. Who needed it? That's what copilots were for.

I looked over at Captain Al, seat pushed back, legs crossed, reading a magazine. While reading, I noticed he was absentmindedly picking his nose, wiping it on his red socks. Good, God! Another one!

At least this guy didn't blow his nose onto the cockpit floor. Frequently looking over, I noticed the *pickin and wipin* just continued. I remember thinking: How much can he dig out of that hole?

A couple of hundred miles or so later, the weather became *rough as a cob*. Al pulled his seat up, wiggling the yoke to indicate, his airplane.

We were on solid instruments in massive clouds pregnant with rain, side cockpit windows leaking all over us. The turbulence ranged from moderate to severe to intermittently extreme.

Ride reports from other aircraft were not good, and most aircraft were deviating from their assigned routes, climbing or descending in attempts to find smooth air. Those fortunate enough to be flying modern jet equipment were often climbing above the weather.

We didn't have that luxury. In fact, we were hoping upon hope for as much lightning as possible to light our way through the worst of it.

The turbulence had progressed to the point where power was increased, and props pushed up to get a better bite of the air. Captain Al soon had his hands full trying to keep that proverbial *shiny side up*, and downdrafts made our forage through the middle of this mess not only exciting but *Son of Exciting, Part Two*.

Suddenly, the nose pitched up with the aircraft rolling left beyond 90 degrees. Al yelled for me to get on the controls. This was followed with, "Get on the rudders."

Looking over at him I noticed he was almost sliding off his seat with his right leg fully extended, blocks or no blocks, trying to right the aircraft and keep it from rolling all the way around. My horizon gyro tumbled. Looking across at Al's gyro, it seemed to be operating but still, didn't look quite right. I am not sure if we went all the way around or not—a complete roll. Once we punched through the line with the turbulence subsiding, I went back to inspect the cargo, as a roaring sound was coming from somewhere behind us.

To my amazement, I found one of the freight skids containing automotive axles had broken the metal strapping. An automobile axle was hanging from the overhead where it had punched a hole through the overhead, between the *stringers*—the area of bare metal ceiling of the aircraft between the main braces referred to as "stringers." It was poking out several inches.

The control cables ran down both sides of the cabin overhead, the axle just missing them. Thank God! I tried to pull it back in but was unsuccessful. I reported to Captain Al that the cargo was somewhat of a jumbled mess and mentioned the axle *slightly* protruding from the overhead.

Al didn't seem at all concerned, as we were through the worst of it. Eventually, going back for a look, he still seemed unconcerned.

Upon landing at MKC, we discovered that the *honey bucket*, a repository of bodily fluids and waste used only in emergencies, had lost its contents all over the aft freight compartment. Luckily, this had recently been serviced with clean disinfectant fluid at the base and had not yet been used. I say luckily because I was assigned to clean it up.

The folks unloading the aircraft took quite a few pictures of the axle poking through the overhead. Unfortunately, we never were given any of the photos. Too bad, as they would have been a nice souvenir. That was one of my most fearful trips. That same squall line we had recently flown through took a Braniff Airlines BAC-111 to the ground killing all aboard. It is not nice to fool with Mother Nature. There but for the grace of God....

We spent the night in MKC, scenarios of what could have been running through my thoughts most all night. Our scheduled departure from MKC wasn't until later the next afternoon.

Before departing for the airport the following day, we had lunch. Captain Al ordered a Coors beer. Takeoff was in three hours!

Coors distribution had not yet extended east past Kansas City.

If you were a beer drinker, for some reason this was thought to be the *"nectar of the Gods," the forbidden fruit* as it were. Crews often loaded up the aircraft with Coors and transported it, illegally, back to Michigan only to discover, in some cases, the Alcohol and Tobacco people were waiting for them, having been tipped off by someone in advance of their arrival. Who did the *tipping* was never discovered. A hefty fine and suspension from the airline usually followed.

Ole Red Socks' reasoning was, *drink it first, and then transport it*. Didn't seem to matter much that he was due to fly in three hours. I turned down his invitation to join him thinking: Not again! Faced with what seemed to be an ongoing dilemma about what to do in these circumstances, I once again decided to keep this more than minor infraction of the FAA regulations to myself as he *seemed* okay! I kept a wary eye on him all the way back but needn't have worried. I was the one that did all the flying, and yes, we still had the hole in the overhead cargo compartment.

Flying Vagabond

19

THE LEFT CHAIR

Many trips and much time had passed before I was selected for an upgrade to captain. Seniority and the needs of the airline dictated everything, especially seniority. Handed a schedule for an upgrade class, I was back in ground school preparing for the oral exam and check ride. My type rating check ride was conducted by *two* FAA examiners assigned to the airline. A fellow by the name of Van Voorhees was the senior inspector with the more junior getting his captain's type rating at the same time just before me.

The safety captain was Bob Hammond, another of the good guys whose patient instruction served me well for the ride to come.

I don't remember the other FAA inspector's name. He was the one who eventually would award me the rating upon the successful outcome of *his* type rating.

Everything went well during my check ride until final approach to the west runway at Toledo, Ohio.

With the newly type-rated FAA dude in the right seat conducting the ride, he reduced power to idle on an engine simulating an engine failure with the aircraft on a close in final approach with full flap.... WTF? This was a particularly dangerous thing to do close to the ground, getting everyone's attention.

Not only was the engine power reduced to idle, but the prop was not set properly to simulate nearly as possible, a feathered engine—thus, reducing drag. As I immediately advanced full power on the good engine, applying opposite rudder against the torque, I could no longer properly control the aircraft. The aircraft departed the straight in course to the runway and was slipping below the glideslope.

Calling immediately for a reduction in flap, the aircraft slowed perilously; the drag of the improperly set *dead engine* propeller exacerbating the situation.

Yelling I could not hold course, altitude, or speed, I attempted to push the dead throttle forward to takeoff power. This new examiner was tightly holding it completely unaware of impending doom.

Captain Bob Hammond was yelling from the back of the cockpit..." ZERO THRUST, ZERO THRUST!" The propeller control had been placed in 'zero pitch," which mimicked a barn door creating a substantial amount of drag to the aircraft.

When this did not immediately happen, Captain Hammond, exhibiting the moves of a scalded cat, pushed Van Voorhees out of his way, reached up and shoved the offending engine throttle fully forward regaining full thrust and nearly breaking the moron's fingers. This quickly relieved not only my sore and aching leg muscles but my severe anxiety as well.

Recovering the aircraft, we landed at Toledo with a great sigh of relief. Once clear of the runway, Captain Hammond unloaded on this FAA jerk, screaming, "You fuckin near killed us, you asshole! Just what the fuck are you trying to prove?"

There were so many expletives filling the cockpit that I could hardly hear the taxi instructions from ground control. Taxiing back for takeoff, we departed for Willow Run Airport.

Arriving at cruise altitude, I overheard Captain Bob say to Voorhees: "You better pass my guy and definitely rethink this other asshole."

I passed! Drinks were had in wild celebration with Captain Bob regaling everyone in earshot of *that idiot fed* who almost killed us.' He generously said:

"God damn good thing Eddie was flying because it really may have happened were it not for quick thinking on his part."

Well, nice of him to say so, but Ole Bob is the guy that really saved the day for all of us.

Flying Vagabond

20

I'M GONNA FLY IT TO THE GROUND!

The hot cargo from the Cleveland Brookpark GM plant was loaded aboard. The aircraft was de-iced as the snow began to accumulate at a pretty good rate.

"Captain, we are filed as Zantop 21 outbound."

"Okay. Starting number one. Call for taxi clearance."

Number one engine started, taxi clearance received followed by a hurried taxi to the active runway while checklists were completed. Having received our airway clearance, Bert announced we were ready for takeoff to the tower.

"Zantop 21, Cleveland Tower, taxi into position and hold runway 23."

"Zantop 21 position and hold runway 23."

"Zantop 21, wind 250 at 15 peak gusts 26, cleared for takeoff. Contact departure when airborne."

"Cleveland departure, Zantop 21 checking in out of 15 hundred for six thousand."

"Zantop 21, Cleveland, Radar contact. Cleared on course. Cleveland center now 128.6. Good flight."

"Good evening Cleveland, Zantop 21 climbing out of four thousand for six."

"Zantop 21 Cleveland Center, climb maintain 6000 cleared on course."

"Zantop 21, Climb to six, cleared on course."

"Christ, we're picking up ice already. Wings already have a heavy buildup on them. Turn the wing boots on Bert and watch 'em. Make sure they are working."

"They are shedding it pretty good so far over here, captain," he yelled above the intermittent cacophonous sound of the propellers shedding ice against the fuselage.

"We can't stay in it for too long. Get a cloud top report."

"Center, Zantop 21 in moderate ice here at 6000. Do you have a top report?"

"Zantop 21, the last top report I had is an hour old. Tops then reported at 15,000 feet. I can give it to you if you want it."

"Tell him no thanks. We're too fuckin heavy, and we have a blower (supercharger for extra power) deferred (i.e., inop). Without that supercharger, we would never make it. I can hardly hold six thousand."

"Did ya tell 'em we are experiencing moderate icing here at six thousand."

"Yes, he knows."

"Holy shit, the props are really slinging ice now. Ask for a direct heading to Detroit Metro. It's closer than Willow Run."

The incessant staccato beat of ice being slung against the fuselage increased the stress level by several orders of magnitude.

How's your wing looking, Bert?"

"It's hard to tell if the de-ice boots are working. I don't see much ice being shed. I think the boots are expanding below the ice buildup. Hell, we aren't going to shed ice from the wings if that's the case," he said, his voice about an octave higher.

"Captain, we could return to Cleveland."

"Too late! It's as broad as it is long now. We're halfway to Detroit," as I pushed the power up to hold six thousand. "Don't know how long we can maintain this altitude."

"Zantop 21, You are cleared direct to Detroit Metro. What are your flight conditions?"

"Center, Zantop 21 is in moderate to severe ice with considerable buildup. We will keep you advised."

"Okay, I have just bumped power to a climb power setting. We'll see if that will hold us at six."

Several minutes later: "Ask for 5000 Bert."

"Zantop 21, Cleveland Center, descend to and maintain 4000."

"That should help. I hope we can maintain it. Get a weather update at Metro and a report for Windsor, Ontario as well. Prop ice is beating the hell outta the airplane."

"Metro's reporting, 'measured 300' overcast one-half mile visibility in heavy snow. Wind is variable at 290 to 320, 15 knots. Runway 22 in use."

"Thanks. I thought that damn front was supposed to have pushed through by now. Musta stalled."

"We're slowing quite a bit. Must have a helluva load of ice on."

"Captain Windsor, met report was zero ceiling, zero visibility in heavy snow."

"Damn, that would have been a good alternate for us."

Advancing the throttles, we were now at METO power (maximum except takeoff).

"Tell center we need 3000 ASAP.

"Zantop 21 cleared to 3000 feet. Contact Detroit approach now."

"Zantop 21 Detroit approach. Information Mike is current. Expect ILS runway 22."

"Declare a fuckin emergency, Bert. Can't hold 3000 without stalling the fuckin thing. Going to takeoff power. It's going to get really noisy." Ask for vectors to final."

"Zantop 21, declaring an emergency. We are in severe icing. Unable to hold altitude."

"Zantop 21, understand emergency aircraft. Fly heading 300 degrees for vectors to final runway 22. Maintain 3000 if able."

"Keep your intercom button depressed. Switch between that and approach frequency when we need to talk to each other."

This all took place while yelling my lungs out to be heard over the roar of the Pratt and Whitney R-2800s—the shedding prop ice adding to the cacophony.

"Run some God damn checklists and set me up for the approach, then brief it. I'm gonna hold the gear till the last minute. Don't need the added drag. Get me a speed for a zero-flap approach."

"Captain, can you see forward out of your windscreen?"

"No! I've used all of the windscreen alcohol already."

"How the hell did those guys fly these things over the Himalayas in these conditions? Christ, I can barely hold 3000."

"Zantop 21, Metro approach, I have you two miles from the final approach fix for ILS runway 22. Turn left heading 260 degrees, intercept the localizer for runway 22 left. Contact Metro tower now."

Metro tower, Zantop 21, emergency aircraft for runway 22 left.

"Zantop 21, Metro tower. Number of souls aboard and fuel in time."

"Two souls, two hours. Requesting men and equipment standing by."

"Roger, men and equipment will be waiting." Caution for snow clearing equipment on either side of the runway. "Zantop 21, Wind

290 at 12. Runway has been plowed and sanded. Braking action reported as fair to good by a DC-7. Runway 22 left cleared to land."

"Tell 'em to get that fuckin equipment well clear. If I lose it on rollout, I don't want a fuckin plow coming through the windscreen."

"Here comes the localizer, captain. Glideslope is above us. How the hell are we going to land this thing with an iced-up windscreen and below the glideslope?"

"An interesting question, Bert! Take the controls and watch the speed. Just fly the localizer. Try to capture the glide if you see it but don't stall the fuckin thing."

"I have the controls. What are you going to do?"

Putting on the smoke goggles, I opened the DV window (direct vision side window) on my side.

Poking my head out, I immediately felt my face freeze. There was no other option if we were to survive this.

Suddenly, I saw the ground. We were very low with full power maintaining only a few knots above stall speed, but we were still flying.

Using visual cues from the side window, I once again grabbed the controls struggling to keep the bitch flying. Intermittently poking my head out of the window, the runway approach lights appeared through the snow. My God, we were low! My face and mustache were freezing with snow and ice buildup. I couldn't feel my nose. Holding the gear extension until the last minute and hoping it would extend, I yelled; *"GEAR DOWN"* motioning for it to be extended. Within seconds, we bounced onto the runway depositing huge chunks of ice that had to be cleared closing the runway for a time. Taxiing to the ramp, I noticed we were both shaking—a very close call indeed.

All in a day's work!

Flying Vagabond

21

WE DON'T NEED NO STINKING PROCEDURE TURN

Not too long after that adrenaline pumper, I was off again to Worcester, Massachusetts with a freight load of about 14,000 pounds. This was one of many trips I had flown to Worcester, MA. KORH.[6]

It was still winter in Detroit. Dumbo was heavy coming off the ground. Upon entering the clouds, our initial rate of climb dropped from 600 feet per minute to 400 feet per minute when carburetor heat was applied guarding against an iced carburetor. This also reduced available engine power.

Leveling off at 7000 feet, we settled in for a couple of hours of monotonous droning of the engines. My copilot had only recently been checked out, and this was his third trip as copilot in Dumbo. Wiggling the controls indicating he should now hand fly the aircraft, I assigned him *autopilot duties.*

Approaching the Worcester area, Boston Approach Control issued a *cruise* clearance, a type of clearance rarely used today. It indicated to the pilot that he was cleared to descend at his discretion to the altitude specified in the clearance.

---

[6] The ICAO airport identifier.

Usually, a *cruise* clearance to 5000 feet always seemed to be issued late by Boston approach control arriving to land at Worcester, invariably leaving you high at the final approach fix.

The procedure, approaching from the south, required a turn outbound to safely establish a stabilized approach inbound to the runway. While safe, certified, and approved, I found it tedious and time-consuming.

On past trips to KORH, the ceiling and visibility had been good. With weather and visibility good, many of the captains I had earlier flown with simply turned in toward the runway. Although they were high, they employed various techniques to increase the descent rate as rapidly as needed to intersect an approximate three-degree glide angle to the runway.

The technique most often employed was beyond the scope of any SOP (standard operating procedure). It involved reducing the throttles to an idle setting while at the same time, pulling both propeller pitch controls fully aft, reducing the propeller pitch to an almost zero state of pitch. This, of course, could be a dangerous procedure, as the aircraft essentially morphed into something that had all the flying characteristics of a greased rock.

If one were visual with the airport, this procedure rarely presented a problem. However, several of my Hump heroes[7] cautioned me against using this technique in instrument weather conditions until I became much more accustomed to the handling characteristics of Dumbo when employing it.[8]

Approaching from the southwest, I took control of the aircraft. Descending into the cloud deck at about 6000 ft., a quick review of the instrument approach chart for runway 11 was made.

---

[7] WWII air transport command pilots
[8] To quote one of them: "It could result in finding oneself joined to another object by an incline plain wrapped helically around an axis, i.e. SCREWED!" I should have listened better!

It stipulated a left turn outbound, away from the airport where a course reversal, called a procedure turn, would be initiated while descending to an initial approach altitude of 3000 feet. Once established inbound to the runway we would have plenty of time to properly configure the aircraft for the approach, thus stabilizing the aircraft for the instrument approach with proper speed, configuration, and descent rates to the runway.

Receiving clearance to proceed directly to the outer marker, the final approach fix (FAF), the approach and in range checklists were completed. Upon reaching the final approach fix, I turned right or inbound instead of turning left, outbound, to a heading of 110 degrees. We were now inbound toward runway 29 and higher than a bull's ass in fly time. The glideslope intercept altitude at the final approach fix was 3000 feet. I crossed it at a little above 4000 feet. Solid instrument flight rules (IFR)—on instruments—in light icing with the wing boot deicers cycling and carburetor heat on, we were high, fast and IFR! Full of piss and vinegar, I was determined to show this new guy *how it was done.*

On instruments with the ceiling reported as 400 feet overcast, visibility one mile in snow showers, I closed the throttles to idle power and pushed the nose over to catch the glideslope considerably below us. The descent rate rapidly increased.

The localizer[9] was captured, the landing gear was lowered. Struggling to slow to maximum flap speed, final flaps were set.

A call to the tower revealed the weather had deteriorated to 200 feet overcast and one-half mile variable visibility with heavy snow—minimum weather conditions for a safe landing. Oh shit!

The runway, while plowed, had a braking action report of only *fair* with plowing equipment moved to either side of the runway.

---

[9] The electronic beam that aligns the aircraft with the centerline of the runway.

My ego had really bitten off a big one this time. Still above the glideslope, I pulled both propeller controls all the way back ala Hump pilot flying, setting zero thrust.

Protesting, the aircraft shook and rattled as the descent rate increased dramatically. Ahhh, here comes the glideslope. Wait, whoops; there went the glideslope! Shit, we descended through it. Shoving the propeller controls forward and advancing the throttles to takeoff power setting, both engines coughed, sputtered, and backfired.

Both engine cylinder head temperatures had cooled reading zero degrees. Placing both throttle levers to a takeoff power setting, introducing large amounts of fuel rapidly to the very cold cylinders, *could* have caused one or both engines to fail.

We were on course but well below the glideslope with indicated airspeed several knots below minimum approach speed and slowing rapidly below minimum control speed as I attempted to arrest the sink rate.

The engines continued to cough and belch. Slowly, they began to respond. The right engine came up first with a vengeance, causing a deviation from the localizer and final approach course. Suddenly breaking out of the clouds, we almost had to look up at the approach lights, which were off to our right and well short of the runway.

An immediate climb was initiated. It was only later that I discovered there was an unlighted 100 feet hill aligned with the runway and was 4500 feet from the landing runway. I don't know how we missed it.

The left engine powered up at that time and now, instead of too little power or speed, we now had too much of both. Reactively pulling the nose up once I saw how low we were to the runway resulted in an overfly of not quite half of the 7000-foot runway. With throttles now reduced to idle power, we slowed beyond which a safe go-around could be attempted. We were committed to a landing.

Touching down with the control yoke fully back to keep the tail wheel on the ground, I applied full braking.

Both wheels locked up commencing a skid. Built way before the advent of anti-skid braking, I pumped the brakes and hoped for the best.

Suddenly appearing through the falling snow were several red lights indicating the end of any usable runway beyond which was a short runway overrun and a rather severe drop-off.

"Holy shit!" We weren't slowing at any appreciable rate!

"Do something dammit!"

During one of several furloughs from the airline, it had been my experience to have been introduced to a *ground loop*.

This occurred on my initial check out in the venerable Twin Beech aircraft, notorious for that adrenaline pumper.

A ground loop is an unintended and often rapid change in direction resulting in anywhere from a 180-degree change in direction to a complete 360-degree turnabout. It was basically a rapid change in direction, sometimes resulting in one or both main landing gears collapsing; less often on dry pavement, more often on a dirt or unpaved surface.

I recall during that check out while landing at Miami International, with too much speed and a brisk wind from our left, the tail of the aircraft swapped ends on me instantly while turning left to clear the runway. A difficult crosswind landing, coupled with the unexpected change in direction, left me flush with adrenaline, hopelessly embarrassed but wiser—much wiser! This was at relatively slow speed, and no harm was done, nor did the landing gear collapse, but it sure got my attention.

I was about to find out if it were possible in a heavily loaded C-46. It was all I could think of to save my dumb ass.

Pushing the right engine throttle to the stops, protesting coughs, sputters and backfires belched as it reached full power.

The aircraft began a rapid turn to the left. Approaching a 180-degree turnabout, I advanced the protesting left engine throttle up to the stops while bringing the right engine throttle back to idle to stop the aircraft from a complete 360 turn.

One hundred eighty degrees was all I needed, and I needed it yesterday! It worked; the heading change being slightly more than 180 degrees, whereupon I restored both throttles to full power, regained directional control and eureka, the aircraft was now moving in the direction from whence it came! No thought was given to the tail wheel, which is always locked in line with the aircraft for all takeoffs and landing. Who said that you didn't have reverse thrust in Dumbo? In retrospect, I wonder what would have become of that tail wheel if the runway hadn't been so slick. Maybe nothing, but I wonder.

The tower saw none of this, as the snow had reduced their visibility.

They did, however, know we used an awful lot of their runway. They asked if we were okay and what would we call the braking action. I just couldn't use that kind of language on frequency. I swore my copilot to secrecy. It was after we were unloaded and before our return trip that the near catastrophic result of that stupid stunt fully hit home.

I spent the next few weeks in a very sullen and despondent mood reflecting upon my stupidity. Eventually, I got over it but have never forgotten it. I have a great deal of very good experience, much of it the result of *piss poor judgment*.

A few years later, at a local crew watering hole, someone mentioned that they had heard a rumor that some stupid bastard intentionally ground looped a heavy C-46 on an icy runway. Had anyone heard that rumor?

I just sat there shaking my head...a stupid bastard indeed.

Flying Vagabond

22

INTRODUCING THE TWIN OTTER

Shortly after the Worcester episode, I was furloughed from Zantop with a promise of a recall to duty in no more than three months. Out of work, I immediately applied to several local C-46 operators only to find no one was hiring.

The economy had slowed to a crawl. A glut of unemployed *freight dogs* (cargo pilots) were looking for work. Hearing a commuter airline based at Cleveland's Burke Lakefront Airport was possibly hiring, I drove to Cleveland. It was called, originally enough, *Air Commuter Airlines* soon to become *Wright Airlines*. With a fresh resume in hand, I sought out the director of operations. His name was Lou Grossman.

Knocking lightly, I was invited into his second-floor office. Introducing myself, I handed him my resume, mentioning that I had heard the airline may be hiring pilots.

Barely looking at it, he turned to look out the large window overlooking the ramp, where there was a rather strange looking aircraft whose right engine was running while loading passengers. Turning back to me, he asked, "Can you fly one of those?" Now that was a familiar question.

Once again, not being too sure as to what one of those was, but with new confidence, I responded, "Yes I can." He replied, "Good, take that one to Dayton and hurry; they are running late." HUH?

Assuming he meant for me to sit right seat (copilot), I hurried to the ramp to board the aircraft.

Passenger boarding was still in progress. Noticing that the aircraft had a very large boarding door for the pilot and assuming there was one on the other side as well, I cautiously walked around to the right side of the aircraft taking great care to stay as far as possible from the right engine propeller that was still running. This aircraft was a Twin Otter.

Opening the door, I was surprised to find the right seat occupied. The startled copilot looked down at me with a look of horror thinking I was an errant passenger. Near panic and fearing I would back into the spinning prop, he yelled and motioned me to, "Get the hell away from the prop!"

Completely confused, I walked to the opposite side of the aircraft and climbed aboard. The copilot, staring and no doubt still thinking I was a deranged passenger, said, "You can't be here!"

I introduced myself, explaining who I was and who sent me.

Shaking his head, he said, "We need to get the left engine started! Passenger loading is completed, and we are behind schedule."

A not too subtle hint for me to get on with it.

Now, the Twin Otter has the engine throttles, propeller controls and mixture levers on the cockpit overhead panel situated for easy reach between both pilots. This configuration was as foreign to me as the space shuttle.

I put on the large headset and sat staring at the engine controls.

Recognizing a thousand-mile stare when he saw one, *my* copilot mercifully started the left engine. Asking how much flying time I had in a Twin Otter, I said, "What time is it now?" He responded with an epithet that sounded like:

"That fuckin Grossman!"

The steering tiller was on the captain's control column. I now had to taxi this aircraft.

To depart the ramp required a right turn.

To steer the aircraft on the ground, the tiller was lifted for a right turn and pressed down for a left turn. Lifting the steering tiller to the right while adding power on the aircraft with the overhead throttles, the aircraft quickly lurched to the right. The ensuing cries of surprise emanating from the passenger cabin were plainly heard through the large headphones.

That rather ignominious beginning was followed immediately by an introduction to a very short, very angry flight attendant.

"Who are you?" she asked.

No time for explanations, I shrugged; she returned to the cabin. The copilot made the takeoff. I was on the way to Dayton, Ohio albeit, in a bit of a daze. Soon after receiving flight instruction in the merits of the Twin Otter, I began to feel more at ease in the aircraft. It truly was an easy and forgiving aircraft to fly.

Flying Vagabond

23

WHAT REGULATIONS?

I had never been asked to produce my pilot's license or medical certificate before being assigned as a crew member that day.

I am not even sure if my total flying time had been noticed on my resume. It wasn't until the early to the mid-1970s that more rigid adherence to CAA/FAA regulations was imposed on the industry. It was during this time that an Eastern Airlines Boeing 727 captain was found to hold only a private pilot's license.

A minimum of a commercial pilot's license with an accompanying instrument endorsement was required to be a copilot in a commercial operation. A multi-engine rating was also needed for all but single-engine aircraft operations. He had been employed and flying as a captain of this large jet for several years, and no one took notice. The nonchalance and often disregard of regulations during the 1960s and early 70s gradually became outdated, thank God!

Air Commuter soon became Wright Airlines. They flew several aircraft from a Cessna 402, Twin Beech 18s, De Havilland Doves and four-engine De Havilland Herons as well as Twin Otters.

The De Havilland Heron.

Twin-engine Convairs were soon to join the fleet. Several months had gone by when I received a recall from Zantop, now Universal Airlines, to return to work. Giving notice to Lou Grossman, I was asked to present my license and medical certificate. Presenting my certificates, he seemed stunned to see that I had an ATR (Airline Transport Rating) license. He said, "Why didn't you tell me you had an ATR? Asking why, he said, "Because you could have been on high pay!"

"And what was that?" I asked.

"$400 a month!" he said.

I had been paid $300 a month. Aw shucks! Despite the lousy pay, it had been a great experience. The commuter airline was my first experience exclusively flying passengers with flight attendants who spoiled the pilots with their attentive service, but it was time to get back to the heavy transports.

24

THE GOOSE

British Armstrong-Whitworth "Argosy" AW-650 lovingly referred to as the "Goose."

Returning to what was now called Universal Airlines, I discovered the new airline owner's edict was all returning crew members were to be paid *new-hire* wages.

Distressed to discover my old seniority number no longer belonged to me, I was assigned another reflecting my new date of hire and recall date.

I was one of many who was livid. The airline was begging for a union. We soon were courted by the Teamsters Union as well as ALPA (the Airline Pilots Association). The Teamsters were very *heavy-handed.*

Some Teamster members under the leadership of the now *missing* Jimmy Hoffa were found to have sugared the gas tanks of automobiles whose owners were known to support joining ALPA. Such heavy-handed tactics were eventually the Teamsters undoing. ALPA became our advocate. ALPA sought to reclaim the seniority numbers of the returning pilots as well as a restoration of salaries reflecting our past years of service to the former airline. Well, it all sounded good but several *years* of negotiations and thousands of dollars of union dues failed to settle our issues.

It was during this time, I had been transferred to the military division of the new airline. Based at Wright-Patterson Air Force Base near Dayton, Ohio, I was assigned to the U.S. Air Forces Logistics Air Command. It was referred to as *Logair* for short.

The aircraft Logair Command was particularly fond of at that time was the British Armstrong-Whitworth AW-650, Argosy lovingly referred to as the *Goose* by flight crews.

The Argosy was a twin-boomed, underpowered, four-engine turboprop. The engines were *boosted* with water injection to increase takeoff power.

A forward cargo loading door swung open as well as a rear cargo door that did likewise. The openings were quite large. With the flight engineer handling the loading, and off-loading, we had six to nine-minute turnarounds from touchdown to *wheels-in-the-well* on takeoff. The Goose was ugly but efficient!

Because of my *new* airline seniority number, I couldn't hold a captain's position, so I began my new posting as a first officer.

Flying for the USAF was arduous, challenging, and a hell of a good training ground.

We had nine flight legs a day, every day that we flew. Flying in all types of weather up to and including zero/zero landing conditions. i.e., zero ceiling, zero visibility.

All instrument approaches flown were GCA (ground-controlled approaches) conducted by USAF radar controllers, issuing course and glide path guidance instructions over our headsets backed up with onboard aircraft instrumentation.

Except for the flight engineer, the flight crew seldom left the cockpit, except to see to physiological needs during the entire nine legs.

The flight engineer left the cockpit after each landing, opening both forward and aft loading doors as necessary as the aircraft was taxied onto the ramp, closing them when loading and off-loading was completed.

Upgrading to the new Argosy equipment presented challenges. At this point in my career, most were easily managed. On one of my first trips from Wright-Patterson Air Force Base in Fairborn, Ohio, I was assigned a trip with a brand-new Argosy captain.

Before an airline captain can be turned loose on his own, he undergoes considerable scrutiny, not only of his flying skills but of his judgment, command authority and overall knowledge of aircraft systems, culminating in a captain's *type* rating in the aircraft. Once having jumped through those hoops, he is sent on his way with both the FAA and the airline's blessing. This usually takes about 25 hours of observation flights (IOE, or initial operational experience) by a designated check captain scrutinizing his every move. The new captain is also restricted to higher than standard landing minimums, which often presented a problem to

Air Force scheduling when the ceilings were too low to land. The pressure and anxiety during this time were often extreme.

My friend Terry had just completed his IOE flights. I was assigned as his first officer.

During initial and recurrent training, there are certain *memory items* that one must commit to memory in the event of an emergency because you must know what to do immediately to resolve a potentially dangerous situation.

Having just completed all his training including the recitation of the requisite memory items ad-infinitum during the oral examination portion of the check, Captain Terry was now considered to be at the peak of his professional ability.

The Goose was notorious for false engine fire warnings caused by the sub-standard Gravenier firewire used in the fire detection system on the Rolls-Royce Dart engines. On this day, the aircraft was loaded to its maximum takeoff weight of 88,000 pounds.

Departing on the west runway at Wright-Patterson Air Force Base was going to require a *wet* takeoff. It was a 90+ day.[10]

As the aircraft reached flying speed with full takeoff power applied, the landing gear was raised. Suddenly, the number four engine fire bell sounded.

The engineer yelled out, "Fire warning on number four!" Now, this is where the captain is supposed to command and *verbalize* the memory items to be accomplished by the flight engineer.

The Argosy being a British aircraft had what are called HP or high-pressure cocks, which when shut, close all fuel and hydraulics, feather the propeller and a myriad of other things.

There are also LP or low-pressure cocks that are also to be closed.

---

[10] Water was injected into the engine to increase air density, thus restoring a certain amount of thrust lost due to the ambient air temperature.

The beginning memory items for an engine fire in this aircraft state were:

"Throttle closed, HP cocks to feather, LP cocks, closed" followed by items to be completed per the checklist by the flight engineer. However, Captain Terry's memory items were:

"Feather the motherfucker!"

The flight engineer repeated, "Roger, feathering the mother fucker!"

Upon closing of the HP cock, the propeller was set to feather,[11] thus securing the engine. The aircraft commenced a gentle but definite descent toward the ground.

All of this took place less than 200 feet above ground. Terry immediately yelled:

"Start the motherfucker up! Start the motherfucker up! I can't hold her!"

Working very fast, the flight engineer relit the engine. Terry immediately advanced the throttle to full power and the aircraft began a modest climb.

Fortunately, there was no fire, but one can't be too careful. One must follow *"Established procedure!"* We did find that *Terry's* procedure was succinct and worked well.

Later that evening, over dinner and a few drinks, we laughed until we hurt recalling his *memory* shutdown procedure.

---

[11] Feathering a propeller turns the propeller to a streamlined position to the oncoming air, thus reducing drag dramatically.

Flying Vagabond

25

RUNWAY IN SIGHT; INSTANTLY, THE WHEELS TOUCH

Flying for the Air Force Logistics Command introduced me to an entirely different aspect of flying. Logair flights for the Air Force, with their Navy counterpart called *Quick-Trans,* were made exclusively to military bases only.

Restricted to only eight hours in a 24-hour period of actual flying under airline regulations (FAA part 121 regulations), we were held to a very rigid flight schedule.

Numbers one and two engines (left engines) were always shut down during taxi in with numbers three and four engines left running the entire day until the final landing. Weather was rarely a factor.

The FAA never seemed to take notice of our *busting minimums* (minimum altitudes for instrument approaches generally were approximately two hundred feet above ground level). We all began to think that we had some sort of special dispensation allowing us to land consistently below weather minimums. Perhaps we did, operating under Air Force Regulations, but we weren't aware of any.

The skill and focus required for zero/zero approaches and landings defy description. Ground-controlled approaches were the standard and crews became wonderfully proficient at them.

On one such approach into Loring Air Force Base near Presque Isle Main, a near zero/zero approach was commenced in heavy snow. We were also experiencing moderate icing in the clouds. Just before reaching the final approach fix on the instrument approach, we were instructed to break off the approach and proceed to the designated holding area.

The approach controller announced that an *ORI* had been called taking precedent to all other traffic for national defense reasons.[12]

An ORI is a surprise inspection, often requiring launching of B-52 bombers and accompanying KC-135 (B-707 type) supporting tankers.

This process can take some time to accomplish. Always greeted with derision by Logair flight crews, they inevitably made a long day longer. With deteriorating flight conditions, this breakout was greeted with more than a few expletives.

Ice accumulation was being handled nicely by the aircraft anti-icing system, but it wasn't something that you wanted to continue indefinitely.

Though our aircraft were well maintained there were times things went wrong. This was one of those times.

Loring Air Force Base was stop number eight for the day with Plattsburgh Air Force Base near Lake Champlain our last stop for the day.

In the holding pattern for about 25 minutes, a red glow was noticed in the clouds. Thinking the glow was from the red anti-collision beacons on top and below the fuselage of our aircraft, the captain called for them to be switched off. At that very moment, the radar controller advised the ORI was over, issuing us vectoring commands for the final instrument approach where we would be turned over to the final approach radar controller.

---

[12] ORI: short for the Air Force "Operational Readiness Inspection."

Becoming very busy with checklists, we failed to notice the red glow persisted after the beacons had been switched off.

Established on the inbound leg of the instrument approach, the captain distracted again by the red glow, asked:

"Why haven't the beacons been switched off?"

The flight engineer responded, "They're off!"

"Then what the hell is that red glow?" he asked.

"Damned if I know," the engineer said rechecking the beacon switches.

The Argosy employed electric *spray mats,* which electrically de-iced a section of wing and tail on a cyclic schedule going from one section to another until all of the wing and tail surfaces had been electrically heated and de-iced in turn. The cycle was then repeated. The four de-icing switches were located on the overhead instrument panel above the captain's head with adjacent small green sequence lights, which would illuminate as each section of the wings or tail were electrically being de-iced.

This instrument approach was to a very low ceiling, and all focus was on getting the aircraft safely to the runway. "Runway in sight." Instantly, the wheels touch. Snowing heavily, the red glow became even more pronounced, now reflecting off the snow as we taxied to the ramp.

While taxiing to the ramp, the flight engineer noticed a green de-ice light above the captain's head had not sequenced properly. This steady light indicated that it was constantly supplying an electrical charge, i.e., heating that section continuously.

Numbers one and two engines (left engines) were shut down per procedure. Opening the aft loading door upon taxi in, the engineer noticed a red glow emanating from the horizontal stabilizer.

Closer inspection revealed a chilling site. Racing to the front of the aircraft, he signaled frantically to the cockpit to secure engines three and four ASAP. They were shut down immediately. Very unusual! The captain, immediately out of his seat, literally flung himself down the cockpit ladder with me close behind. The horizontal stabilizer, which held each aft protruding boom in place, had burned almost the entire way through, the fire having been assisted by the slipstream while airborne. This accounted for the *red glow*. It was, in fact, still burning and smoldering as we taxied to the ramp.

Had we not landed when we did, the twin booms could have possibly separated as the horizontal stabilizer burned through, rendering the aircraft unstable resulting in a certain crash.

We spent the night in the BOQ (bachelor officers' quarters). It was the next day when a replacement aircraft *arrived* and was loaded to continue the previous day's trip, albeit a bit late.

26

THE DESIRE FOR SAFETY STANDS AGAINST EVERY GREAT AND NOBLE ENTERPRISE

—Cornelius Tacitus, Circa AD 56

lthough the cargo loads on most Logair flights were usually rather benign, some flights were quite explosive. Black powder is an explosive powder used in ammunition and bomb-making often loaded aboard in one form or another with a notation of *hazardous cargo* on the manifest—a fact driven home when the aircraft was directed to a *hot spot* for unloading.

The hot spot was a designated and desolate place on the base that, should the aircraft blow up during loading or off-loading, it wouldn't take the whole base with it. Cheery thought that! On one such trip into Tinker Air Force Base near Oklahoma City with an undisclosed amount of black powder explosive aboard, we encountered an area of severe thunderstorm and lightning activity. The worst of it was a bit north and west of Tinker and moving rapidly to the east. Approaching from the northeast, the radar was painting the storms vividly.

To say that you could have read a newspaper or magazine from the light of the radar on the instrument panel would not be an exaggeration.[13]

Being intently focused on the radar screen, a *hook* signature was noticed at our 12 o'clock position on the radar screen—a tornado signature! Tinker was also at our 12 o'clock position but closer than the *hook*. Turbulence and lightning abounded.

Our cargo load suddenly became a mounting concern. I advised that we could divert to Will Rogers Airport, which was much closer. Captain Ron overruled me, reminding me of our hot cargo and scheduling requirements as we literally raced the tornado to the ground. Landing in extreme turbulence with an ever-shifting wind direction, we were immediately directed to the hot spot where we had to wait out the storm, which was soon upon us.

Fortunately, the twister touched down a few miles to the north and west of us. However, we still experienced cloud to ground lightning in all quadrants with heavy rain and gusting winds shaking the aircraft violently.

Both the flight engineer and I had more than a few words with our captain over this incident. One lightning strike and any future children of mine would not have been born.

---

[13] Thunderstorms on aircraft radar often blossom, their radar echo return shining brightly in the cockpit.

27

LIFE ISN'T ALWAYS FAIR, BUT IT DOES HAVE ITS MOMENTS

After months flying the Argosy, regulation required the passing of a pilot proficiency check ride. Normally, this was done with a designated company check airman with certification authority.

On this day, however, Universal Airlines' principal FAA operations inspector chose to ride along. The purpose was a periodic check of both the company check airman and his checking of me. While waiting at the aircraft for the check airman to arrive from operations, the FAA inspector and I stood talking about what was expected of me during the proficiency check ride.

By this time, I had logged hundreds of hours in the left seat as *acting captain*. I asked if I took my check ride from the left seat and completed the required maneuvers for a captain's rating, would he award me a *type rating* in the aircraft.[14] I had already passed a required oral examination on the aircraft.

He agreed that he would do so. However, the final authority rested with the agreement of the company check airman. The argument was made to the check airman that I was already a captain

---

[14] A "type rating" in an aircraft is a license that shows that you have passed the rigorous testing requirements and qualifies you to fly as captain in a particular aircraft.)

in a different company aircraft and that he, the FAA inspector, was amenable to granting me the type rating if he, the company check airman agreed. He didn't!

His reasoning was that I was a first officer on this aircraft and he didn't care what seat I took the ride in, he was the company check airman. He was not going to agree to the granting of an FAA type rating on a first officer's check ride, period.

A captain's rating in an aircraft does not mean that one will fly captain for the airline.

It means that an individual has met and passed the standard testing required to be a captain should a need arise later.

For some reason, the *fed* (FAA examiner) agreed with the airline check airman to my chagrin.

I have never forgotten the disappointment nor forgiven the jerk check airman who refused that simple request. Years later, while waiting for an elevator at the Woodland Hills Marriott in California, the door opened and much to my surprise, there stood that same Universal Airlines check airman, then a captain with Air California, now American Airlines, with several of his crew members crowded in behind him.

His name was Al, (not the same red socks Al mentioned earlier). I said:

"Hello Al, remember me?"

It was apparent that he did not until I said:

"I was at Universal Airlines, flying as first officer on the Argosy when you were company check airman on the Argosy."

"Oh yes. How you are doing?" he said.

I doubted he remembered me until I said: "I'm the guy that you refused to allow the FAA to type rate during my first officer's check ride several years ago. I haven't forgotten that, nor had I forgotten you."

With a startled look of recognition, he looked away, brushed past me, and passed out of my life once again without another word.

I don't know what he thought, but I enjoyed seeing his discomfort in front of his crew as they looked at one another. I am far from a vindictive person, but I must say, that felt good.

Flying Vagabond

28

DON'T FORGET THE FUEL!

One spring day a few years later, on landing at Wright-Patterson Air Force Base, all arriving company aircraft were advised on the company radio frequency to refuel and return to the home base: Detroit's Willow Run Airport.

This was unusual and ominous. Getting the word from our operations after landing, one of our sister Argosys was taxiing out for takeoff as we taxied in.

It was procedure to call operations 30 minutes out from landing. They had not done so, thus were surprised at the news. Waving off the fuel truck, they departed without refueling. It was later discovered the flight engineer had advised the captain the fuel state was low; "It would be very tight fuel-wise." The captain overrode him. Long story short, they never made the Willow Run Airport, landing on an interstate highway just outside of Toledo, Ohio. They were out of fuel and passed over several cars with all four propellers in the feather position. Zero drag! The aircraft was equipped with an *auto feather* feature in the event of an unexpected engine failure. The FAA descended!

One of the men who had been in the meeting with Captain John Palmer on that fateful day years before that I had rudely interrupted was the chief engineer for Zantop, now Universal Airlines.

His name was John Roberts. John was a no-nonsense, fast-talking and astute individual. With more than a little prestidigitation, he convinced the FAA the aircraft should have had more than enough fuel to make it with reserve fuel and on that assumption, the experienced captain while perhaps imprudent, should not be faulted for taking off.

As to why they didn't make it was never fully explained. Both pilots and the flight engineer had their certificates suspended for several months, and the captain was fined an undisclosed amount.

29

DEJA VU ALL OVER AGAIN!
BACK IN DUMBO!

Arriving at Willow Run, we were advised that all company personnel were to proceed to our large maintenance hangar where a podium had been set up.

With over six hundred pilots and flight engineers, flight attendants and maintenance personnel in attendance, the hammer dropped! Universal Airlines had ceased operations that afternoon.

We were all now unemployed as of that moment. I had been furloughed before from Universal but only for a short time and always recalled. There was no recall from this. Several years of great experience and good times had ended.

There were many freight operators still on the field. I immediately applied to all of them. Shamrock Airlines operated several aircraft, three C-46s and two DC-6s. Hired by them, I found myself back in Dumbo.

After passing a difficult captain's recurrent check ride after not having flown it for quite some time, I was once again a qualified C-46 captain.

Initially based at Willow Run, I soon discovered that I was seldom there. Instead, I was spending time in temporary bases such as Lexington, KY flying the occasional racehorses to JFK for transport overseas. I was also assigned TDY (temporary duty) to San Juan, PR. Flying between Caribbean Islands with assorted cargo loads, never getting much over a hundred feet above the water, was just fantastic. To say this was great flying and wonderful duty would be an understatement. NO SNOW! Occasional trips back to the States were flown picking up such things as unsewn ladies bras and baseballs, mostly from Hattiesburg, MS and flown to Haiti where for about eight cents an hour, the natives would do the finishing stitching. We would then fly the finished product back to the States for distribution.

Shamrock C-46's on the ramp at San Juan

Many wonderful months passed—great weather, great flying, and great fun.

My old friend and C-46 Captain Bob Hammond from Zantop days was now also a C-46 captain with Shamrock Airlines and was permanently based at San Juan.

Invited to Captain Bob's home for a cookout, I was surprised to learn that his house lacked a backyard as such. He used the flat roof of the garage, attached to the front of his house, as his patio. Extending forward of the house, reaching almost to the street, it was the perfect patio.

The house was small with barred windows. Theft was a problem in San Juan at that time, and most all houses had barred windows.

Captain Bob and his wife Betty were perfect hosts—good food and lots of beer. About an hour into our *backyard* cookout, we heard an accented Spanish voice yelling, "Bub, Bub!" (Bob with a Spanish accent). Looking down to the driveway there stood Bob's neighbor yelling excitedly, "They are in your house! They are in your house!"

Bob said: "Who's in my house?"

There was a slight pause. "I don't know their names! he cried emphatically, but they are in your house!"

The house was being robbed while we were enjoying a quiet afternoon at a rooftop cookout.

Bolting toward the house with me in close pursuit, we charged down the stairs. Hearing us coming, the thieves dove through the window at the rear of the house where they had skillfully removed the bars. Running flat out, they hopped over several fences and were gone in a flash. Lying about on what grass was in the tiny backyard was a TV, several lamps and kitchen items.

To break and enter when you aren't home is one thing, but to do so brazenly while you were, was unbelievable.

Eventually, I was reassigned to Detroit Willow Run Airport. Taxiing onto the ramp at Willow Run, I noticed two small corporate jets on the freight ramp. They were strange looking aircraft. The wings appeared to be attached backward. These were German Hansa Jets.

It turned out that one of my former crewmates from Universal Airlines was a captain on one of them. He told me the aircraft were owned and operated by Lloyd Zantop of Zantop International

Airlines whose new offices and base were now at Detroit's Metropolitan Airport.

"Would you be interested in flying for Lloyd? He has four of these Hansa Jets and is looking for pilots!" Not knowing what they were and not bothering to ask, I immediately responded:

"You betcha!"

30

THE HANSA JET

The next day, I was in Lloyd Zantop's office. Interviewed and hired in less than 10 minutes, it was with the proviso that I successfully complete the required schooling and pass the FAA captain's type rating for the Hansa Jet.

The schooling consisted of one day of system instruction administered by a Hansa Jet pilot sent from the Hansa Jet corporation located at White Plains Airport, NY. A grand fellow by the name of Ed Wiester was assigned as my flight instructor. An experienced Hansa Jet captain, he had been tasked to get me trained ASAP.

He provided a few hours of flight training consisting of takeoffs and landings in various configurations and an assortment of simulated engine failures.

Lloyd Zantop had a great need for qualified pilots. I overheard him saying to Captain Wiester, "Just get him ready to pass the type ride. We can teach him what he needs to know beyond that later." No pressure there for Ed Wiester or me!

Below is a picture of serial number 1025, the last flyable Hansa Jet that has been lovingly restored in Hamburg Germany where it was built. Only 47 were produced.

The aircraft presented an unusual design. The forward sweep of the wings improved the aircraft's [15]stall characteristics, ensuring that the stall occurred at the wing root (nearer to the fuselage) making it more predictable and allowing the ailerons to maintain full control.

The Hansa Jet.

The Hansa was ahead of its time using composite material. To compensate, the wing tanks had a slight downward *twist* to reduce the angle of attack—the angle at which the wing meets the airflow at the tips increasing *tip lift*.

A potentially dangerous consequence of this increase in tip lift under load is a tendency to tighten into a turn (rolling further into an un-commanded roll while turning) even if the pilot is not trying to do so—a surprise to the unwary.

---

[15] A few words about that: A forward sweep wing is an aircraft wing configuration in which the quarter chord-line of the wing has a forward sweep. A wing stalls when it can no longer provide lift due to a reduction of necessary airflow resulting in a reduction in speed.

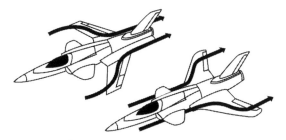

The inward span-wise flow

As you can see from the above illustration, span-wise airflow over a forward-swept wing is the reverse of that produced by a conventional rearward-swept back wing. Air flowing over a forward-swept wing tends to move span-wise inboard toward the rearmost end of the wing toward the wing root. On a rearward-swept wing, this is outward toward the tip. With the air flowing inward, wingtip vortices and accompanying drag are reduced. The fuselage acts as a very large wing fence. Since wings are generally larger at the root, this improves lift, allowing a smaller wing.

This improves maneuverability, especially at high angles-of-attack. Shockwaves build up first at the root rather than the tip, ensuring more effective aileron control.

The Hansa Jet design was years ahead of its time, but it had some problems; the major drawback was the engines. The Hansa Jet was a hell of a lot of fun to fly—just a bit underpowered.

The only engines available at the time of its manufacture were the GE CJ-610, a General Electric non-afterburning turbojet engine. Its maximum thrust was only 2,800 pounds. Various versions of the CJ610 have powered business jets such as the Learjet 23, 24 and 25 models. [16] The Learjet's maximum weight for takeoff was only 12,499 pounds. The Hansa had a maximum takeoff weight of 20,280 pounds.

---

[16] It was also used to power the Messerschmitt ME 262 reproduction aircraft built by the ME 262 project in the United States.

You can see the problem, but the GE-610 was the only small turbojet engine available at the time. They were grossly inadequate to power the heavier Hansa Jet but more than adequate for the much lighter Learjet.

Despite this single disadvantage, the Hansa Jet, once airborne, was a delight to fly. Longer takeoff runs, however, were the rule rather than the exception. Often asked about the performance of the aircraft, I would say: "Performance was pretty good because of an onboard RES." The inevitable response was: "Oh I see.... What's a RES?"

"A runway end sniffer!"

It seemed no matter how long the runway for takeoff, at max loading it would seek the runway end before lifting off. That made for more than a few exciting takeoffs.

The Hansa Jet, FAA designation HFB-320[17] was not only a unique aircraft because of its odd wing design, but it was also among the very first small jets to be employed as a corporate aircraft. The German military were among the first to employ them as executive transport aircraft.

---

[17] Hamburger Flugzeugbau, a Hamburg aircraft factory

31

JET TRAINING IN THE AIRCRAFT ...HMM!

Training in the Hansa Jet was memorable. One event stands out. While practicing touch and go landings at Willow Run Airport, a not particularly dangerous exercise as long as rather quickly after landing, the landing flap is retracted to a takeoff setting, and aircraft trim is reset for takeoff.

After completing several touch and go's, we were going to practice one more and stop for the day.

On landing, I advanced the throttles to about 80% takeoff power while Ed was to retrim the aircraft for takeoff, setting the flaps to the takeoff position. Advancing the throttles to full power, on his command, at the previously computed speed, we lifted off. Unfortunately, on this last landing, Ed failed to bring the flaps to the takeoff position. Landing flap was still selected. This added several hundred pounds of aerodynamic drag to the aircraft. Not recognizing his mistake, Ed reduced power on one engine to idle thrust simulating an engine failure at liftoff.

With flaps in the landing configuration, the remaining engine could not produce enough thrust to overcome the drag of the flaps and sustain flight. At the end of this runway stood the GM Chevy plant and we were heading for its second floor! Because of the slow speed of the aircraft and not wanting to risk stalling the aircraft, I was unwilling to turn or bank the aircraft very much, thus reducing lift. The building loomed ever larger in the windscreen. Screaming that I could not hold the aircraft, we were descending rapidly toward the Chevy plant. I had to turn.

Ed immediately recognized the problem, reduced flaps to the proper setting and immediately pushed the retarded engine throttle to full power. We cleared that building by several feet in a now very steeply banked turn. I swore I saw a few terrified faces peering through some of the windows as we roared overhead. I made Ed promise not to do that again.

After three or four hours of flight training, one day of systems ground school, and several hours spent studying the aircraft flight manuals, I found myself on the way to Cleveland Hopkins Airport where the FAA inspector waited.

32

A CHECK RIDE OUGHT TO BE LIKE A SKIRT, SHORT ENOUGH TO BE INTERESTING BUT STILL LONG ENOUGH TO COVER EVERYTHING!

The FAA district offices were located above Sundorf Aviation in a nondescript building located on the north side of Cleveland Hopkins Airport.

Sitting for an oral examination covering aircraft systems and limitations, memory items and weight and balance procedures was, to say the least, *stressful!* The oral lasted about two hours followed by a flight check in the aircraft lasting a full three hours. Clearly, this test was a *bitch*. The examiner was very tough, demanding I demonstrate every instrument approach and emergency procedure he could think of. Single-engine training in a multi-engine aircraft is inherently dangerous, the reason flight simulators proliferate today. Thankfully, a stressful three hours later, with the flight check passed, I was awarded a captain's rating in the Hansa Jet. This remains the longest and toughest check ride I have ever experienced.

Later that night, with only a few hours' sleep, I found myself flying the Hansa Jet to San Jose, California from Detroit. The aircraft, limited in range, required three technical stops for fuel.

After several years flying below 15,000 feet, this high-altitude flying at 30,000 plus feet was a new experience.

The stress of the check ride coupled with the stress of flying a new type of aircraft left me seriously fatigued. Fortunately, my copilot was a seasoned Hansa Jet first officer so, sliding my seat back, I proceeded to check my eyelids for leaks.

Soon, not fully asleep, the sound of the landing gear being extended announced our arrival at our first fuel stop. After an uneasy nap, the rest of the flight proved unremarkable.

Eventually, the Hansa Jet became a very comfortable aircraft for me to fly. My initial anxiety of high-altitude flying waned as experience grew.

33

AHHH, THE ROCK GROUPS!

I'm filled with many memorable experiences flying the Hansa. Most flights were cargo flights with about 25% being passenger flights. Often assigned to fly rock groups from city to city during their tours around the country, we often stayed with them for weeks and in a few cases, months. Groups such as Emerson, Lake and Palmer, Fog Hat, Three Dog Night, The Carpenters, and Kenny Rogers and The First Addition were among several that I had the pleasure to fly during their respective tours.

Crews were periodically changed out after being on the road for extended periods. Sometimes, the group managers would request a crew to remain with them throughout their tours. "The Carpenters" and "Three Dog Night" being just two of the groups I had the pleasure of flying on extended tours.

I was the primary pilot for the Carpenters band during a several city tour, occasionally flying Richard and Karen. Karen was an absolute delight, but I found Richard less than friendly.

He seemed sullen most of the time and non-communicative. Karen was just the opposite. When Karen passed, the world lost a wonderful songbird whose voice was unequaled. During the tours, Karen and Richards's manager left no doubt who was in charge. His trucker belt buckle had the word *BOSS* inscribed in bold two-inch letters. Karen's weight seemed always to be an issue with him. I felt sorry for her. I wonder who he is bossing now.

The clarinet player in the band, a fellow by the name of Doug Strawn, was quite amusing, entertaining us with his "Donald Duck" voice. His was better than the Donald Duck voice we usually hear. Years later, when the original voice of the *iconic Donald* passed, I heard that Doug had auditioned for and became the new voice of Donald Duck.

I spent some memorable moments with Donald Duck during a very low-ceilinged instrument approach. The clouds were literally on the ground. Donald (Doug) was standing in the cockpit during the approach (only slightly illegal) looking out the forward window as we broke out of the clouds at a very low altitude. *Doug* was heard to say in his unmistakable *Donald Duck* voice, "Holy shit," followed by that Donald Duck laugh. You haven't lived until you have heard Donald Duck say, "Holy shit!"

A well-deserved weekend of rest in the Shenandoah Valley, Virginia after a concert nearby was most welcome.

Doug did not stay at the hotel with the rest of us. Renting a car, he was off to visit his sister's family, less than an hour's drive away. They had not seen each other since the birth of his niece. Upon his return, he had a remarkable tale to tell.

Doug's sister, a first-time mother, had just given birth to a bouncing baby girl. After a long evening of catching up, Doug was shown to his bedroom adjacent to the baby nursery. The proud parents' bedroom adjoined the nursery on the other side.

Extinguishing the light, burrowing comfortably in the covers, his bed suddenly shook a bit. It seemed to stop abruptly. Thinking no more about it, but mildly curious and getting comfortable once again, the bed shook, this time with more vigor. Unnerved, he reached for the light. Not seeing anything that could explain the shaking and thinking perhaps a mild earthquake may have been responsible he silently vowed to mention this in the morning.

Mystified and a bit disturbed, he once again turned off the light only to be shaken once more, this time more violently than the last.

Springing from bed, reaching for the light, finding no reason for the shaking and mumbling to himself, he bolted into the hallway toward his sister and her husband's room.

Passing the open door of the baby's room, which was lit in the soft glow of a night light, he could see the baby. Looking in, he discovered to his horror, a mound of sheeting about its neck. She was turning blue. Yelling for his sister and brother-in-law, he quickly unwrapped the sheeting from the baby's neck. She didn't seem to be breathing. He immediately started small chest compressions and gentle mouth to mouth.

The baby was revived!

A man of many talents, he was also a volunteer fireman and had been schooled in life-saving arts. Relaying what had brought him to the baby's room, they all proceeded to Doug's room, inspecting every corner and nook. Finding nothing, and after quite a bit of head shaking and wonder, everyone had a good night's sleep, even Doug, as the shaking had finally ceased.

Now, there are those who will believe this to be a story of divine intervention and those who will just view it as a lucky chance. Either way, it brings the hair on my neck straight up!

My favorite group, however, was the *Three Dog Night*. Great guys all. The band was terrific; the music, unforgettable. The after-concert parties were as wild as you might expect where *every* fantasy was often indulged.

The old saying of "sex, drugs, and Rock-n-Roll" pretty much says it all. I have never seen so many ladies willing to give so much to so few.

On a few flights, I did have to insist that smoking marijuana on the aircraft was an absolute no-no! Only one band member had to be constantly reminded not to "toke" up during flight. I never witnessed any of the three singers in the group smoke anything at all. The *Dog* was still touring until recently but without Chuck Negron who made the song "One" so popular. He had left the group.

Unfortunately, in late October of 2015, Mr. Cory Wells passed away. He was one of the original three of The Three Dog Night and sang *Jeremiah Was a Bullfrog* among many others.

34

YOU GOTTA BE SHITTING ME!

Back to flying freight after the rock groups was anti-climactic and not nearly as much fun.

Late one night, a call was received from Ford Motor Company dispatching a Hansa Jet to Cincinnati's Northern Kentucky Airport (CVG). *Hot cargo* destined for the Ford Motor plant in Detroit was waiting. Labeled *HOT,* it was needed ASAP to prevent a very costly assembly line shutdown. I was assigned the trip.

Starting the engines for the outbound leg of the trip, I noticed that the number one engine (left side) took a bit longer to start than usual but otherwise seemed normal. The number two engine had started without difficulty.

Arriving at CVG, the aircraft was quickly loaded.

Attempting to start the number one engine once again produced no engine instrument indications of an engine start. Several attempts to start it failed. That was not a good sign! Number two engine had once again started normally. A call was placed to operations in Detroit.

Lloyd Zantop answered the phone. Immediately understanding the implications of lost revenue, he said: "I'm not asking you to do anything you are uncomfortable with" I remember him saying, "but if there is any way that you can think of to get that engine going, please try it and get back up here."

I said I didn't think so, as I believed the engine starter may have *sheared* the starter shaft on the first startup in Detroit. I assured him I would keep trying. The inference was clear, however.

The jet engine is an air breather. I thought that if enough air were introduced into the engine with a high-speed run down the runway, it just might provide enough engine rotation and with constant engine ignition on, it just might start.

The longest runway at CVG was 10,000 feet long, adequate to make an attempt.

Another runway intersected the takeoff runway at 90 degrees at about the 5000 feet point. Should the attempt fail, that is where I would abort the takeoff attempt.

I presented this idea to my first officer. He remarked, "You gotta be shitting me!"

Explaining our failsafe options, he reluctantly agreed.

Number two engine was started, and a takeoff clearance was requested.

What I had not considered was the excessive asymmetrical torque of the operating engine at full power. Keeping the aircraft heading straight down the runway proved more than difficult.

Somehow, I managed. Accelerating slowly through 80 then 100 knots, more speed was needed. Still no *light off* of the engine as the agreed upon *abort* point approached.

"Just a little bit more. Gotta keep going," I heard myself saying as we crossed the abort point. Lifting the nose as the aircraft continued to accelerate slowly, we were suddenly airborne. Reaching about 100 feet of altitude, the nose was lowered to increase speed.

The resulting increase in airflow through the engine spun the turbine to self-sustaining speed, the fuel was ignited, and a most welcome sound was heard as the engine spooled up to full power. The tower operator, suspecting something not quite right with our initial slow climb and acceleration, asked if we were okay.

Charlie, my first officer, ever the quick thinker replied, "No. We are okay!" The Skippy (his favorite name for me) is due for his six-month check very soon, and we are just practicing a bit.

Approaching Detroit Metro Airport, I called Zantop operations on the company radio frequency and advised that we would be landing in 20 minutes. A rousing cheer was heard over the frequency. I did not have to pay for drinks for a long while after that. Lloyd took good care of us.

Not everyone was pleased with this escapade, however.

Several pilots expressed their displeasure over what they called an over the top stunt while a few more felt it less a stunt than a successful attempt at getting the job done. My former Hansa Jet instructor pilot, Ed, mentioned that had this been wartime, we would have been awarded a medal.

Nearly 20 years later, after landing at Teterboro, New Jersey airport, there stood one of Lloyd Zantop's former pilots. He was among those most vocal and angry in his displeasure regarding that infamous takeoff, I was surprised and happy to see him. Him, not so much.

I got a, "Hi, how are you?" as he quickly walked toward his aircraft—not a welcome reunion at all. Okay, I get it, but 20 years had gone by and still this animus? I can only feel sadness and compassion for him. His seeming lack of respect for me was disappointing. He seemed to be burdened by some sort of grudge. Grudges are a heavy burden, eventually weighing one down physically, mentally, and spiritually. I must say, I have been accused of many things through the years, but carrying a grudge has never been one of them. It's a waste of energy. I wish him well.

Flying Vagabond

35

OH NO, NOT AGAIN!

The following winter, I experienced an engine failure in the Hansa Jet at liftoff departing from Detroit's Willow Run Airport.

The weather was terrible this night with very low ceilings, icing and blowing snow. Surface winds were 15 to 25 knots 40 degrees to runway heading.

Cargo had been waiting for shipment to San Jose, CA. I had been assigned the trip.

Operations advised that an aircraft already in position at Willow Run was being fueled and loaded. A treacherous drive to the airport left me once again anxious about takeoff conditions.

The freight load consisted of heavy metal castings for the automobile industry. Loading was completed, weight and balance computed; we were ready to go. Immediately after de-icing the aircraft, we taxied quickly to the takeoff runway. Low ceilings, restricted visibility, snow showers, blowing snow coupled with high gusty winds were going to make for a very challenging takeoff.

Runway braking action was reported as fair to poor. Four and five-foot snowdrifts on either side of the runway, the result of the recent plowing and blowing snow, gave the runway a tunnel appearance.

Takeoff clearance received, the throttles were advanced smoothly to the stops applying full takeoff power. Accelerating slowly at first and skidding slightly into the crosswind, the aircraft reached rotation speed.

Gently pulling back on the control column, the aircraft lifted off. A positive rate of climb was called, I commanded, *GEAR UP!* Almost immediately the right engine failed.

Both airspeed and rate of climb diminished appreciably. Declaring an emergency, the tower controller acknowledged our emergency and asked our intentions.

I answered, "Get the airplane safely on the ground somewhere!"

I was informed that Detroit Metro Airport was a few miles in front of us but was currently closed because of runway plowing in progress.

We could be vectored over to that airport but were told it would take a substantial amount of time to clear the plowing equipment. Willow Run Airport, however, was open but well below landing minimums at 100 feet variable overcast and one-quarter mile visibility. In an emergency, all bets are off. An immediate decision was made to return to Willow Run.

We were radar vectored to the ILS approach for runway 23. The aircraft was not handling well at all. Emergency checklists completed, the instrument landing system frequency was tuned. The glideslope portion of the instrument landing system was flagged red indicating that it was not available. Questioning the controller, we were informed that the glideslope portion of the instrument landing system was "NOTAM'D" (notice to airman—out of service).

Now, this may have been an oversight on our part, but in fairness, these notices are generally checked when you're landing at an airport not when you're departing an airport. Not expecting to immediately return to land, we had not checked these notices. Electronic runway guidance, referred to as the localizer, was working and would keep us lined up with the center of the runway.

A very strong crosswind from the right, however, was making that problematic. An ILS approach is made up of an *initial approach fix* (IAF) and a *final approach fix* (FAF). As we crossed the IAF, we asked the radar approach controller if he had vertical guidance approach radar capability, sometimes referred to as a PAR approach (precision approach radar) a ground-controlled approach.

"Negative," was his response. We were on our own!

An accumulation of ice buildup was noticed at the windscreen side posts. All anti-ice capability was switched on. Extreme icing of the one remaining engine was disconcerting, as this could potentially cause an engine flameout of the only operating engine resulting in game over! We needed to get on the ground…now!

Upon crossing the final approach fix, a 700 foot per minute rate of descent was established toward the runway. At approximately 100 feet, the runway lights came into view, and we were slightly low. Power on the remaining engine was increased to full throttle. The nose of the aircraft was raised increasing drag while decreasing airspeed.

The landing was made on the runway approach overrun with the aircraft stall warning operating. Due to poor braking action, we used a fair amount of runway before stopping.

Taxiing the aircraft back to the ramp proved to be difficult with only one engine providing asymmetrical thrust on a slick surface.

Parking and securing the aircraft, a post-flight walk-around inspection was performed paying attention to that right engine. The aircraft had accumulated a considerable amount of ice during the instrument approach.

Upon inspecting the right engine, several of the turbine blades appeared to be misshapen, indicating something had been ingested. I strongly suspected ice ingestion, as the engine failed immediately after gear up was commanded. A chunk of ice, possibly thrown loose from the nose landing gear as it retracted, deposited itself into the right engine intake. This caused a flameout of the engine. My copilot asked if I had been as frightened as he had been. Calmly responding and still flush with adrenaline, I said, "No. Why do you ask?" I had been a smoker in those days.

"You have two cigarettes going."

I had one in each hand!

Looking back on that event, I probably could've done things better, but I am equally sure that what I did was good enough to get us safely back on the ground and in one piece, but just barely.

Zantop Airways also flew three Learjet 23 aircraft and a Learjet 25. Lloyd now thought I would make a good Learjet captain, so I was off to school again. Within a week, I became the newest Learjet captain at Zantop Airways.

36

THE CORPORATE ADVANTAGE, OR DISADVANTAGE!

It was 1973. Gas lines stretching for miles were forming across the nation. The oil embargo was in full swing. A shortage of oil was blamed. Approaching the East Coast and from a height of several thousand feet, I saw groups of heavily-laden oil tankers riding low in the water waiting their turn to offload thousands of gallons of crude.

The problem was, there were no available storage tanks, as they were all *full*. HUH? Where was the media in all this? Surely, they had to have known. I am certain that there were many other factors influencing this crisis that we were not privy to, but a shortage of oil didn't seem to be one of them.

Soon, the price of gasoline began to spike, eventually reaching the point of obscene profits for the oil companies in collusion with big government. The cost of a gallon of gas finally stabilized, for a while, but at a much higher price than before the "crisis."

Before long, gas prices slowly began to rise once again, peaking at a high of five dollars plus for a gallon in some places. One oil company executive during an interview said (paraphrasing here) that people in Europe had been paying much higher prices for years, implying that we should consider ourselves fortunate that it had taken so long for those higher prices to reach our shores. What unmitigated greed!

Oil prices have recently taken somewhat of a dip thanks to the oil boom in the Dakotas and the advent of *fracking* practices nowadays. An oil glut seems now to exist. However, even though the price of a gallon of gas stabilized for a time, I have no doubt they will once again be on the rise.

The automobile freight business began to suffer, as automakers' sales dipped to record lows. Unsold gas guzzlers filled dealer inventories. The economy faltered; the outlook was bleak. Lloyd Zantop laid off a few pilots. A few were asked to stay on with a small retainer and a promise of reward for loyalty when things returned to normal. I was one of those.

Many months passed. Lloyd began selling off aircraft to stay afloat. Two of the Learjets were sold. A Hansa Jet was also sold to Associated Theaters in Pittsburgh, PA.

A provision of the sale of the Hansa was training for the crew. I was one of those assigned the task of crew training.

A few months after training had been completed, the new owner of the Hansa Jet called to say that both of his new pilots had quit and did we have anyone who may like a change of employment given the state of the automobile freight business. I volunteered.

It was my first foray into the corporate aviation world, and I liked it. It was much cleaner than freight with far fewer restrictions.

Our family was off to Pittsburgh Pennsylvania to begin my new life as a corporate pilot.

Summoned to the downtown offices of Associated Theaters, it didn't take me long to figure out that this job was less corporate and more private flying for the owner, Mr. Ernie Stern. The pay was adequate. However, the expenses while on the road soon proved to be a point of contention with Mr. Stern. He was miserly, to say the least, and insisted that we eat only in fast food restaurants while on the road such as Burger King, etc. He happily said, "Don't worry. Submit all receipts, and I will see you are reimbursed." I protested to no avail and came away wondering what I had gotten myself into. No wonder his first crew quit.

This proved to be a very large cause of disagreement for both myself and the new copilot. It didn't take very long before I was completely disenchanted with Mr. Stern and Associated Theaters.

On one trip returning to Pittsburgh's Allegheny County Airport from the Bahamas, a frequent destination, the right engine generator failed on descent followed several minutes later by the left engine generator failing.

The weather was marginal with low ceilings and visibility. The aircraft batteries were now the only electrical power source powering our emergency flight instruments, and they were failing fast. An emergency was declared. Now receiving priority handling, we were vectored for an immediate ILS approach to Pittsburgh's Allegheny County Airport.[18]

Visibility was reported as one mile in rain with a 300-foot overcast. With the ship's batteries failing rapidly, the flight instruments were becoming increasingly questionable. The inbound course heading to the runway was 271 degrees.

With the veracity of the emergency flight instruments now in doubt, I determined that flying the inbound runway heading and continuing the approximate 700 feet per minute rate of descent to be the best course of action. An audible sigh of relief came from my copilot as the runway was sighted directly at our 12 o'clock position and about a mile in front of the aircraft.

Once parked, a close examination of the aircraft revealed long black streaks on both engine cowlings. When opened, both electrical

---

[18] The instrument landing system is the only approach available utilizing emergency flight instruments.

generators on each engine displayed signs of extreme heat caused by the internal failure of the electrical brushes of both generators.[19] Stern, when noticing this, asked: "Why did you break it?" Not what I expected!

I made a call to Zantop's director of maintenance explaining the incredible coincidence of both generators failing almost simultaneously.

He quietly informed me upon the sale of that particular aircraft, he had been instructed to remove both *good* generators from the engines and replace them with old worn out ones that still had some life in them. At the time, generators were approximately $30,000 each. I asked, "How much is a life worth?"

Stern just wasn't a very nice guy. To bring his character into perspective: we had landed one evening after a long trip with Ernie's wife Reggie on board. I overheard Ernie instructing her to be at the airport the next morning at 10 o'clock sharp, as we were taking off for Freeport in the Bahamas.

He emphasized several times she needed to be there at 10:00 AM, or he would leave without her. I thought that a little strange, as I assumed they would ride to the airport together.

The next morning, it was a few minutes to 10:00, and she was nowhere in sight. Arriving 15 minutes sooner, Ernie said, "Start the engines." The engines started, and at the stroke of 10:00, Ernie said, "Let's go!"

I released the brakes and started taxiing slowly toward the runway. Out of the corner of my eye, I spotted his wife's Rolls-Royce coming through the gate and stopped the airplane.

I said, "Here she comes, Ernie!"

"Fuck her; keep going!" he replied.

---

[19] Without the brushes of an electrical generator contacting slip rings of the rotor, electricity can no longer be produced.

The last I saw of her that morning was Reggie waving frantically for us to stop. Nice guy!

It wasn't long before Ernie decided it was too expensive to fly the jet, so now we were going to fly in his other aircraft. He had two other aircraft. One was a Handley Paige Jetstream and the other a Howard 500 unpressurized, a modified Hudson bomber circa WWII era.

I was instructed to *familiarize* myself with the Jetstream, as that was what we would now be flying primarily, and while I was at it, do the same with the Howard 500 aircraft. I explained I was not familiar with either one of those aircraft. He replied:

"Find so and so at the airport. He can check you out."

I took a few training flights with so and so, who turned out to be Captain Bill Lloyd of GC Murphy Company who also flew a Jetstream aircraft. Soon, I was checked out and ready to go in the Jetstream.

Warned the French Aztazu engines were very unreliable on the Jetstream, I was advised caution should be exercised while flying it, especially as this aircraft received little maintenance.

The Jetstream was a single-pilot aircraft. Deciding one day to practice some touch and go landings to become more familiar with the aircraft, the right engine exploded during my very first solo takeoff. The immediate asymmetrical thrust very nearly caused me to depart the runway to the right. The tower advised they had seen flame from the right engine and dispatched the firetrucks.

Once the fire was out and it was safe to move the aircraft, it was towed back to the ramp. The runway needed sweeping. There were several engine parts strewn about.

This is known as a catastrophic engine failure. A call was made to Mr. Stern advising him of this unfortunate event. His response in a very angry voice was:

"What were you doing flying the aircraft without my consent," and once again:

"Why did you break it!"

I put him on notice immediately that I would seek employment elsewhere. He slammed the phone down! Securing the aircraft, I went home and advised the family that we may be facing another move, as I had just given notice at work.

No sooner had I mentioned this than the phone rang. It was Stern, his tone now softer and mellower than the previous conversation.

He asked, "Would I please proceed to my offices downtown? I have something very important to discuss with you."

Arriving at his office the next day, I was informed he had been working on a deal to lease the Hansa Jet to a real estate company based in West Palm Beach Florida. Would I be interested? Would I! I couldn't wait to get away from this guy.

It was explained, that should I decide to accept this offer, all moving expenses and salary were to be paid by the real estate company, Deer Run Holding, based in West Palm Beach Florida.

Contact numbers and principal names of the officers of the holding company were supplied with instructions to contact them. I couldn't wait to make the call.

37

SOMETIMES, YOU EAT THE BEAR. SOMETIMES, HE EATS YOU!

—Anonymous Old Appalachian Proverb

Deer Run Holding Co. was primarily a father/son real estate company based in Tennessee but operating out of West Palm Beach Florida. The aircraft would be used to fly clients on weekends to Tennessee where they had extensive land holdings.

These holdings were located near McMinnville, Tennessee and for sale as future home sites.

The nearest airport was a small field servicing the town of Tullahoma, Tennessee. Salaries were agreed upon and a new copilot hired. My former copilot from Associated Theaters had found himself another job.

I hired another fellow with some jet experience. No official schools existed for the aircraft, so the schooling, training, and familiarization were all completed by me.

He was a quick study and proved to be a good pilot. Soon, we were flying every weekend to Tullahoma with as many as 8 to 12 passengers on board as well as one of the principles of the company.

Things went well at first. Everyone was pleased with the aircraft, and they were selling property. A rosy future was in the offing.

As the aircraft flew primarily on weekends, I suggested that we attempt to recruit another corporation or corporate manager who might like to share time on the aircraft to offset costs. Through a network of friends, I heard that Pepsi-Cola Bottling of Miami might be interested. Meetings were held. Financial arrangements were concluded between all parties. Both myself and my first officer were paid in cash each time we flew a trip for Pepsi.

General Cinema Corporation owned Pepsi-Cola Bottling of Miami. General Cinema Corporation's home offices were in Boston Massachusetts. Trips for Pepsi Bottling were flown during the week and always to Boston.

Soon, it was revealed that General Cinema Corp. did not approve of the Pepsi Bottlings CEO having a corporate aircraft at his disposal. The CEO of Pepsi Bottling told us that it was none of their business, as the financial contract agreements were between him personally and Deer Run.

Everything went along fine for a few months until several of our paychecks for trips flown for Deer Run bounced due to insufficient funds. I called Deer Run.

Told to resubmit them again for payment, we did. The bank once again refused to honor their checks. Contacting Deer Run again with this latest refusal, I was advised that they promised they would take care of it. This happened several more times over the course of the next few months with an on again off again payment schedule.

It wasn't long before both my first officer and myself were owed several thousands of dollars. We were still expected to keep flying. The fact that we both had families was ignored. One Friday evening, I received a call that a *must fly* trip was going the next morning to Tullahoma with several high-paying clients. Told to get the aircraft ready for an early morning departure, the phone went dead. I called them back.

Asking for our back pay, I was advised there was no pay available now, and they would address this issue when we returned.

Enough was enough! I drove to the airport, opened the aircraft and removed several of the black boxes, things such as communication and navigation radios along with other essentials necessary to fly the aircraft, after placing a notice on the door of the aircraft stating:

"This Aircraft Unsafe for Flight!"

Signing my name and ATP number (airline transport pilot) I sealed the door with tape and placed the radio equipment in the trunk of my car.

Driving to the main airport terminal at West Palm Beach, I placed them into 25 cent lockers. Then, driving to their offices, I once again asked face-to-face, for our back pay.

The father and son owners of this venture became belligerent and red-faced. They both stood up yelling across the desk:

"We don't owe you a fucking thing!"

As I stood to leave, I replied: "When you decide you do, I will return your aircraft to you!"

Thinking that I had flown the aircraft somewhere to hide it, senior reached for the phone calling the Sherriff as I beat a hasty exit. I called my first officer telling him what had occurred and told him to go into hiding. I was afraid we were now in big trouble, which in fact, we were.

As it turned out, had I not flagged the aircraft as unsafe, things could have gone much worse for me than they eventually did.

A call was made to the CEO of Pepsi Bottling in Miami telling him that the aircraft we have been flying was no longer available to fly his trips, explaining why. He asked if we could procure another aircraft. My first officer was rated in a Hawker Jet and said he knew of one that was for lease. I was not captain rated in the Hawker, and in fact, had never flown one. A call was placed. Arrangements were made to meet with the individual who had the aircraft to lease in Indiana. A meeting was set for the next evening in Indianapolis, IN where contracts and all documents were signed with authority granted by the CEO of Pepsi Bottling. Money was wired, the aircraft hastily inspected, and we were soon on our way back to Miami.

I had been in contact with my wife and was advised there was a warrant out for my arrest.

She said, "Do not return to West Palm Beach!"

She advised she would procure an attorney to represent me. I was also told the sheriff's department was literally camped out on the front lawn of our house. They had also staked out the airport hoping to snare us in their net.

Taking up residence in a hotel near Miami airport we were supplied with cash by the CEO of Pepsi Bottling to buy what we needed in the way of sundries and clothes. He was in sympathy with our cause, plus, he needed us.

One week later, an attorney called. Hired by my wife to represent me, he said I should immediately return to West Palm Beach and turn myself in. Informed he was familiar with my case, as it was all over the front pages of the West Palm Beach newspaper, he asked:

"Where are the radios."

I said, "She didn't tell you? They are in a couple of lockers at the main terminal building in West Palm Beach airport!"

Being watched constantly by the sheriff's department, she had enlisted the aid of one of her girlfriends to keep the flow of quarters going into the lockers.

He said, "The radios must be returned at once." He then asked for the locker numbers. The next day, my first officer and I flew the Hawker aircraft from Miami airport to West Palm Beach airport.

Surrounding the aircraft as we parked, we were greeted by the Palm Beach Sheriff's Department. Deplaning the aircraft, I was immediately pulled to the ground and handcuffed as I came down the steps. A tall, distinguished looking gentleman who had been standing near the aircraft yelled at the officer who threw me to the ground. Threatening to have him brought up on charges of unnecessary roughness, demanded all belligerence be halted immediately.

"No one is resisting here," I remember him saying.

He then introduced himself to me. He was my new attorney.

I was taken to the sheriff's headquarters, and I was interrogated while being tape recorded. I wasn't frightened, concerned of course, but not frightened. I felt that what I had done, while perhaps illegal, was morally right. In retrospect, I suppose there are many people in prisons today that feel the same way.

Eventually released on my own cognizance, I was advised within two days' time there would be a hearing held to show cause for my arrest, trial, and possible incarceration.

Arriving at the courthouse days later, I was surprised to find quite a crowd of people. Many were reporters and correspondents from the local newspapers and television stations asking me questions and snapping pictures as I walked toward the courtroom. This highlighted the gravity of my predicament in my mind. It slowly dawned on me that I could be sent away for a long time. Oh shit!

Seated across the courtroom were the father and son plaintiffs and seated next to them were five gentlemen: their battery of attorneys.

Apparently, they could pay their attorneys, just not their pilots. My attorney, who was a former FBI agent, was all by himself and as events unfolded, he was all we needed.

The door to the judge's chambers opened and out walked the judge. We recognized each other immediately. On more than a few occasions, I had coffee with this judge at the Palm Beach Airport where he was a student pilot. He was familiar with the Hansa Jet, as I had given him a tour of the aircraft one day. He was also quite familiar with how often it flew. At the time, I had no idea he was a judge.

Turning to the plaintiff side of the courtroom he said that he was familiar with me and would be happy to recuse himself from the hearing, explaining to all, his past association with me. All parties on both sides agreed to keep him on. Complaints were read.

My attorney called his first and only witness. It was the company secretary. She had been responsible for writing our paychecks. During a rather long course of questioning, the question was asked:

"Did you write the paychecks for the pilots when they were to be paid?"

"Yes," she replied.

"When you wrote these checks to the pilots, were they written from a large company ledger containing blank checks?"

"Yes," she replied.

"And when you wrote those checks, did you subtract the amount of each check from the preceding balance, and then enter the new balance below it?"

Now the answer to this question was expected to be; "Yes." Instead, she answered:

"No."

My attorney, who was walking across the courtroom at the time of the question, spun around in surprise. He asked her to repeat her answer. She once again replied:

"No, I didn't."

The attorney once again repeated the question, and once again the answer was:

"No, I did not."

He asked her why she did not do that.

"There was no balance to subtract from!" she replied.

Now, you can imagine this created quite a stir in the courtroom. For clarification, the question was put to her once again, and once again the answer was:

"No."

My attorney addressed the bench:

"Your honor, now, and in view of this young lady's testimony, it would be appropriate to advise the plaintiffs they are liable for possible criminal prosecution."

The judge then stood asking both sides to join him in chambers. Several minutes later, all parties filed back to their seats. The judge was ready to give his ruling.

A warning and severe admonishment to opposing counsel with possible further repercussions were administered.

He then stated that he saw no reason for me to be placed in custody and asked me to approach the bench. He stated that while he understood and even sympathized with my actions, he wanted to make it eminently clear those actions were illegal and potentially dangerous to my future.

He mentioned that had I not placed the sign on the door of the aircraft, it would have been even more egregious, safety now an even larger issue.

Explaining had I been an aircraft mechanic, a *mechanics lien* using possibly the same technique I employed, would have been legal, as there were laws on the books that covered such a lien and ensuing actions. It did not however, include pilots. He then advised me where I could file a civil suit against the plaintiffs.

The hearing was adjourned. I made my way to the civil suit office where assisted by my attorney I filled out the necessary papers to file suit against my former employers. My attorney's fee; $1000 dollars. My copilot did not have money. The attorney accepting his motorcycle in lieu of cash. I had to borrow the money. Remember, we hadn't been paid.

I was called the next day by Mr. Ernie Stern who had been aware of the events concerning his aircraft and asked if I would fly the aircraft back to Pittsburgh. I refused. I don't know how it got back and I don't care.

By the way, it took two years to reach a judgment on the civil suit.

I won! However, the day the judgment was announced, the owners of the company took the Deer Run Holding Corporation into bankruptcy. The same day I won the suit, I lost the suit. I received nothing. *Sometimes you eat the bear. Sometimes, he eats you!*

38

THE HAWKER TYPE RATING

After the dust settled, trips on the Hawker for Pepsi bottling of Miami resumed but were becoming less frequent. General Cinema Corp. had grown increasingly disenchanted with their Miami chairman's *unauthorized* use of a corporate aircraft for his personal pleasure. The aircraft lease was to be terminated.

Not wishing to seem ungrateful, but recognizing it was now or never, I asked permission to use the aircraft in acquiring a captain's type rating in the furtherance of my flying career, explaining the aircraft was necessary to demonstrate my piloting skills in several emergency situations as well as my judgment and command presence during the handling of those emergencies.

His generous permission was granted. Not long after, I was a new Hawker Jet captain. The lease was canceled, the aircraft returned.

Full-time Hawker Jet captain jobs were scarce, especially for a new captain who was a little light on captain experience in that airplane.

I did find that temporary *contract* flying jobs were more abundant. Soon, I was doing well as a Hawker Jet and Learjet contract pilot, most as first officer on the Hawker and captain on the Learjet.

39

I'VE FLOWN IN BOTH PILOT SEATS. CAN SOMEONE TELL ME WHY AN IDIOT OFTEN OCCUPIES THE OTHER ONE?

A few weeks passed when I had been offered a contract trip on a Lear 35 out of Dallas Love Field for a company whose chief pilot had been flying without a medical certificate and had been dismissed.

The company's only remaining pilot, the first officer, had been upgraded to the vacant chief pilot/captain position. They needed someone to fly *right seat*.

Available and hungry, I took the contract job. It wasn't long before I discovered this guy could barely *taxi* the Learjet safely let alone *fly* it.

Instructing him for four days during several flight legs had no appreciable effect on his flying or taxiing skills. It was apparent he resented my *babysitting* as he referred to it. He had a small mind and a big mouth and just didn't know when to open one and close the other.

Upon our return to Dallas, I was offered the chief pilot position by the company CEO who had recognized their error in promoting him.

They were going to keep the other fellow and provide him to me as my copilot. I didn't want any part of it. He was belligerent, arrogant, hardheaded, a lousy pilot and unsafe to boot. The cockpit of any aircraft is much too small for conflict between crew members. As bad as I needed a job, I wished them luck and returned home to West Palm Beach, Florida

40

THE ODYSSEY BEGINS

I flew contract assignments for several months. During that time, I literally saturated the industry with my resume.

Some companies will often hire a pilot, pay him much less than he is worth and expect him or her to be grateful, loyal, and quiet. I worked my ass off to get where I thought I was and deserved a fair wage.

One day, the phone rang, and to my delight, another lucrative contract flying job was offered. Once again, flying the venerable Learjet 35 at $500 a day (great pay for that time) and a return airline ticket to PBI. I leaped at it. The trip: MIA (Miami) to SEA (Seattle).

Arriving at Miami International Airport, I found the FBO (fixed base operator) and my contact person. The call had come from the supposed owner of the Lear who, over some disagreement or other, had fired his pilot on arriving in Miami. Not too smart, as home for him was Seattle. He had gotten my name from another pilot at the FBO in MIA *after* he suddenly realized that he had kind of screwed up.

This was a very big guy, about 6'4 or 5, looked mean as hell and was a former logger. He now owned the logging company. My copilot, David, had worked for this fellow only a short time and had very little flying experience. This was his first jet aircraft. He was grateful for the opportunity just to be in the right seat.

On the trip back to SEA, I was briefed on what had happened with the pilot, and what was about to happen to him and to my surprise, what had already happened to the Learjet.

I had been aware the previous pilot had been fired, but was unaware the copilot was about to be, and that the Learjet had been sold. Holy cow!

I had been hoping for a possible job with this guy and his company, so this was not exactly welcome news. However, welcome or not, the short-term money was good. If I could continue to keep the wolf at bay, pay my bills, and eat regularly, all was well with the world.

Upon landing at SEA, a business associate of my passenger greeted us. I was told a room had been reserved for me at the airport's Red Lion Inn and that further instructions would be sent the following morning.

I had expected to return almost immediately to PBI, however, if it meant more flying at the same daily rate, this could work out.

At this point in my career, I had worked for three *non-sked* cargo airlines (FAA Regulation Part 121 carriers), two corporate operators (FAA Regulation Part 91 operators) and had been repeatedly furloughed and had both corporate operations fold when they saw the first fuel bills or simply because they were dishonest. Suffering through a few layoffs at the airlines may have actually been better than working for the many *flakes* that were wealthy enough to own their own jet aircraft. I hadn't yet been introduced or exposed to any of the better corporations that owned and operated jet aircraft, at least none that were willing to hire me. Flying for a Fortune 500 corporation is much different than being the personal pilot of the guy who *owns* the corporation. Being the CEO's pilot can be a good thing or bad thing depending on whether he is a control freak, one who demands that you bend rules, violate safety, and simply say *yes sir* to his every command and desire.

It was much better to be employed by one who views your expertise as a highly-specialized skill requiring many hours of intensive training, testing, dedication and diligence, and someone who treats you as a professional and a source of trust, well-being, and comfort. As one CEO put it, "My family rides with you. How much more of an endorsement is required."

Now, that's my kind of CEO. Rare, but they are out there. Unfortunately, so are many of the other types.

The next morning, I was informed that I would be *deadheading* (no passengers) to New York's LaGuardia Airport where the new owners of the Learjet would meet me. Perhaps a job was in the offing after all.

Landing at LaGuardia is always a challenge, but when the weather is down and the runway slippery, the word *challenge* simply doesn't cover it. Winter had descended on New York. A job or a ticket home to West Palm Beach was all I wanted at this point.

The landing proved a bit dicey but overall, uneventful. Taxiing to the Marine Air Terminal, now dedicated exclusively to corporate aircraft, I thought of its proud history. It had long ago served as the embarkation point for the huge Pan American Clipper flying boats of the 1930s. Through the doors of this Terminal passed the great, near great and famous celebrities and politicians of a bygone era.

We were met by three men, all brothers, all dressed alike in long black topcoats with upturned collars. Each sported black, short-cropped beards. They were from somewhere in the Middle East. The suspicion of Muslims and radical Islam had yet to evolve. These three men were polite, soft-spoken, and friendly. They greeted us both warmly and with respect.

"Captain *Edie*?" one of them asked as the cabin door was opened. I replied *Eddie* and whereupon *Edie* was repeated. I thought it humorous and admitted that I was *Edie*. A business card was offered, which read: *FADI SHIPPING*. I was informed that a hotel room had been provided for us both at the Pierre Hotel on 5th Ave: would we both please be in their offices at the listed address the following morning at 8:00 am? Fadi was located just a few blocks up from the Pierre on 5th Ave, at the General Motors building.

Fadi Shipping's offices were located on the 10th floor. Announced and ushered into an office that was several times larger than all the rooms of my home combined, there sat one of the three brothers half-hidden behind an enormous desk. Aladdin, the older and obviously the one in charge, was seated with Benjamin and Hussein, the other two brothers standing behind. We were to learn that there were two other brothers who we were yet to meet.

After pleasantries were exchanged, Aladdin asked, "Captain Edie, could you please take the Learjet with us to Athens?"

"Georgia?" I responded. "I would be happy to."

"No captain; *GREECE!*"

I had never been across the ocean at this point in my career.

Appealing to my sense of adventure, I blurted out: "When do you want to leave?"

My newly-acquired copilot, Dave, said, "Not me!"

Aladdin said that was fine, paid him several hundred dollars for his service and wished him well. Would he please stay for a day or two longer, as it may be necessary to reposition the aircraft?

A paid ticket would be provided to return to his home at such time it was decided his services would no longer be required. David agreed to this.

Turning his attention back to me, he asked, "Could you, in the space of three days, acquire all of the things necessary to make such a trip, including a new copilot?" I was sure that I could. Hell, I didn't really have a clue. One thing in my favor was a network of friends and aviators that I could call upon. Everyone *networks*.

I asked if Fadi Shipping enjoyed a Dunn & Bradstreet rating. Assurances were given they were well financed.

Explaining there were many expenses involved in preparing for such a trip, much through credit that would only be given by assurances of excellent standing in the business community. Of course, I was also thinking of myself in this regard.

After some discussion, agreements were reached regarding mine and any future copilot's salary. An additional $200 a day was added to my daily rate of $500. I was ecstatic.

I was provided with a company "black American Express card" and told it should be used only as necessary. I had already been added as an additional signatory with American Express. Things were moving very fast.

Acquiring trans-oceanic navigation charts was first on my list. We needed European and Middle Eastern navigation charts as these folks were obviously Middle Eastern. Jeppesen in Colorado was not much help in the chart department, as they wanted money up front (no problem) but would be at least a week or longer providing me with the requested coverage. I couldn't wait that long. Second on the list, I didn't know a thing about this aircraft in terms of its latest inspections and maintenance history. I had to discover what I could of the maintenance history of the Learjet.

Perusing the logbooks, I discovered the Lear was out of inspection needing a minor 'A' check—a minor check required little time to accomplish. Thankful that it was all it needed, and after explaining my predicament, Garrett Aviation on Long Island agreed to fit me in ASAP.

Next; a copilot and charts. After several calls, I was given the name of "Windstar Aviation" based, I believe, at Republic Field, Long Island.

Windstar Aviation was the singer John Denver's company. Much later, I came to know John Denver when I was based at Aspen, Colorado and thanked him personally for his company's generosity.

I can't remember the captain's name that I spoke with, but after listening for several minutes, he agreed to send a flight bag containing a complete, up-to-date *Worldwide Coverage* of Jeppesen navigation charts to my hotel. He also provided me the name of a very experienced pilot with many ocean crossings under his belt.

He knew this fellow was available, but I should hurry in calling him, as he was a very busy contract pilot. He thought he might be current in the Learjet 35 and by the way, would I please return the navigation charts when I finished with them. Holy cow! Here was a guy who didn't know me from Adam but was willing to help a fellow aviator in need. God bless him. I sure wish I could remember his name.

Things were falling into place nicely. David said goodbye once the aircraft was flown to Garrett Aviation on Long Island. He was provided a ticket back to his home in Seattle. In the meantime, calls to my prospective copilot were received with enthusiasm.

Arrangements were made upon his request to have a minimum of four days' remuneration wire transferred to his account before he agreed to take the trip. Why didn't I think of that?

Four days had transpired since my first meeting at Fadi. Finally ready to depart, I met Roger, my new copilot, who arrived at Garrett Aviation by limo the day before. Roger was many times more experienced than me with many captain type ratings on his license. I was somewhat intimidated by him but soon got over it. I was careful to check and double check everything that I could possibly think of.

Still, I fell short as Roger set to work arranging flight plans, flight following, and handling. I was aware that I needed to do these things but was unsure as to how. Roger knew, and after a few calls to Universal Aviation in Houston, Texas, we were ready.

Snow had begun falling the day before our planned departure from Long Island. All day, through the following night, it snowed and snowed. I was worried this storm might delay our departure. After speaking with Universal Weather, Roger and the three brothers, a decision was made that we would make a final go or no-go decision at our proposed departure time.

As our predetermined departure time neared, the snow seemed to abate a bit.

The brothers arrived via limo after several hours' crawl through the terrible weather. Discussions of delaying for better weather was discarded. We were going.

Our departure date and time, as well as our decision to go, had now been set in stone. Our departure time from the East Coast was coordinated for a pre-planned arrival time in Athens, Greece including all planned fuel stops along the way.

Neither Roger nor I were happy with the rigidity of that schedule given the weather conditions. However, we had both been down this road before at some time in our careers, and it worked out…. "Soooo, let's give it a go, shall we?" I said. Ahhh, the young and the brave!

During fueling, bags and passengers were loaded. Fueling took place in the hangar, which was entirely out of the ordinary, but given the weather that night, it seemed like the best plan.

The fuelers happily agreed after a little *green* incentivized them. The good folks at Garrett had no problem with my fueling request and graciously refused any attempts at bribery.

Finally, being tugged from the hangar, the Learjet was almost immediately covered with heavy wet snow. Towbar unhooked, a quick spray of de-icing fluid, the engines were started. A *hurried crawl* to the runway was undertaken. Completing checklists during taxi, we now had to find the runway. Receiving airway clearance, radios were tuned to tower frequency. On reaching the runway, we were immediately given takeoff clearance. "Now, *this* is what I call a shitty night," Roger said, stating the obvious.

Heavy snow began once again falling at record rates. A forty-degree crosswind was peaking at 30 knots. Visibility was as low as 600 feet in blowing snow.

Instruments were checked, the runway heading checked, brakes were released, and the Learjet started an immediate but slower than usual acceleration toward takeoff speed.

I had briefed Roger that due to some snow accumulation on the aircraft I was going to *hold it on* for an extra 10 knots above rotation speed in hopes that the machine would fly. We could barely see the wings. The sanded runway centerline was obscured by snow. Heavy snow filled with moisture *should* slide off the wing with a reasonable speed. At least I hoped it would.

Roger called *rotate.* Hesitating slightly, letting speed build, I gently pulled back on the control column, rotating the aircraft. The Learjet lifted off. I called for the gear to be retracted. We accelerated through V2 (minimum safe climbing speed in the event of an engine failure) reached climb speed, and we were on our way! This was the proverbial "dark and stormy night."

Thus, began a life-changing odyssey, memories of which still linger in haunting and sobering moments of retrospection.

41

ACTION, ADVENTURE, ADRENALINE, ANXIETY!

O nce airborne, we settled in for a several hours' flight to Gander, Newfoundland, a technical stop, and the jumping off point to enter the trans-oceanic part of the trip.

Calling the controlling authority to activate our trans-oceanic flight plan, we were advised that Gander was zero/zero. (zero visibility and zero ceiling).

"What are your intentions?" the controller asked.

We asked for the current weather at our alternate airport of Goose Bay Labrador.

The answer: zero/zero!

Once again, "What are your intentions?"

Asking for weather for Halifax, Nova Scotia, and St. Johns proved equally as disappointing. Both were behind us at this point.

Now, I wasn't sure whether what I was feeling was my sphincter muscle contracting or was it just that it was a little late in contracting.

We proceeded to our filed alternate airport of Goose Bay, Labrador. Goose was a combination military and civilian airport.

I asked if a GCA (a radar ground-controlled approach) was available and was advised it was. We would be at a minimum fuel state arriving at Goose and needing to land...period!

Our request for a GCA approach was passed on. Turned over to approach control, we were informed by our initial radar controller that our request for a GCA approach was granted. Frequencies were checked, instructions given, vectors received. We were turned onto the final approach to the runway. Clearance was issued to contact the final radar controller. With instrument landing system frequencies tuned in as backup, radio checks completed, the approach began. Immediately, constant steering and vertical glide path commands commenced. Moderate icing on the approach added to the stress.

My experience with GCA approaches while flying contract for the Air Force served me well on this approach. Roger had no previous experience with this aberration and enjoyed it thoroughly.

The GCA controller was one of the best. He guided the aircraft right down the center line of the runway. The last instruction from the ground controller during this type approaches is, "Over landing threshold, take over visually" at which point, you should see the runway well enough to *gently* land the aircraft. It had generally been my experience in the past that when the weather was reported as less than landing minimums, we rarely saw it until the moment of touchdown.

That was the case with this landing. A *VERY* firm landing was made at a rather high rate of speed. (Adrenaline!) Unbeknownst to us and during the instrument approach, the older brother, Aladdin, was sitting close behind us in the cabin. At the time of touchdown, a very audible gasp was heard from him as well as a long sigh of relief from the cockpit.

At well over 12,000 feet, the runway, thank God, was very long with a 'fair' braking action.

I was gaining a good deal more experience on this trip than I had anticipated. Funny thing about experience, it is always something you need just before you get it, but once you get it, your good to go till next time…generally.

We refueled and then had the aircraft sprayed with de-icing fluid. Flight plan clearance to Shannon Ireland was requested and received—a technical stop for fuel.

Leveling at FL410 (41,000 feet), we settled into the routine of route checking, position reports, time between fixes and fuel state. It was very clear at altitude when off to our left, the northern lights made an appearance, beautiful, majestic, and quite active with multi-colored light shards shooting off into space. I had never seen them before and was awestruck. They were unbelievably beautiful!

Flying Vagabond

42

FLYING IS LIKE SEX—I'VE NEVER HAD ALL I WANTED, BUT OCCASIONALLY I'VE HAD ALL I COULD STAND

—Stephen Coonts

The technical stop in Shannon, Ireland proved uneventful. We were soon on our way to Athens, Greece. Several hours later, the Peloponnese peninsula came into view. It was now daylight. Both Roger and I were just about at the end of our personal range and were very happy to see it.

Arriving on the ramp in Athens, the engines were shut down, the door opened, and there stood two bearded young men wearing long black coats accompanied by an armed security detail.

Speaking in Arabic, much kissing and hugging commenced. Introductions were made. "This is Captain Edie, our pilot." These were the other two brothers, now totaling five in all.

Roger was affixing the engine inlet covers when the oldest brother, Aladdin, shouted for him to stop. I mentioned we were securing the aircraft for its stay on the ramp when he said:

"No captain. Now we go to *DAMAS*!"

I could've sworn he said, *dumb ass*, and asked him to repeat. Once again, "*DAMAS*" was repeated.

This time I got it, but darned if I knew where *DAMAS* was. It turned out that DAMAS was Arabic for Damascus, Syria. The fact that we were dead tired was ignored. We were told that Damascus, Syria was only a short trip from Athens and that we could rest there. Hotel arrangements had already been made. Now, frankly, I had no idea whether Damascus was up down or sideways from where we were standing, and neither did Roger.

The best thing we could think to do was to find a flight service station, as they are called in the States. I had no idea what they were called in that part of the world. We needed to file an international flight plan to "DAMAS."

Neither Roger nor I were wearing pilot uniforms, just sports jackets, ties, and slacks. We soon discovered that was a lousy idea.

Several months before our arrival in Athens, an El Al Boeing 707 airliner had been hijacked from Athens to Edi Amin's Entebbe near Central Africa. All access to the aircraft ramps was strictly forbidden without proper documentation. Entering the building from the ramp to file a flight plan, we noticed two armed guards placed on either side of the door as we entered the terminal building. They were armed with what appeared to be Uzi machine pistols. Eying us suspiciously, they stopped us immediately asking for our identification. One of them spoke English. After lengthy questioning and examination of our documentation, we were allowed to proceed.

After many inquiries, the correct office was found, and a flight plan was filed.

Returning to the same ramp access point where we had previously entered stood two different guards equally well armed. We were denied access. Exhibiting our passports, our filed flight plans and even our pilot's licenses were of little use in getting past these two very large, armed guards. Neither of them spoke a word of English. Oh hell!

Fortunately, an employee of Olympic Airways, the Greek national airline, happened to be passing. Witnessing our predicament, he stopped to assist. His English was impeccable. He explained who we were, pointing to the Learjet on the ramp. He explained that we were the pilots and that we would like to get back out on the ramp to our aircraft as our passengers were soon to arrive. The whole time this conversation was taking place both guards had their fingers very close to the triggers of their Uzis. It was translated for us that *pilots* wore uniforms! Why weren't we?

After a rapid-fire conversation between our translator and guards, we were finally granted access to the ramp and our aircraft. Mental note: Get some bloody uniforms *ASAP!*

This was just the overture to a string of future events involving Uzis, AK-47s, bayonets and excessive adrenaline.

Flying Vagabond

43

SYRIA

Our passengers soon arrived accompanied by those two fellows who had been guarding the door. There was now a total of seven passengers. The Learjet is tight when you have five passengers, but seven made it downright uncomfortable. One of the passengers was Senator Joseph Montoya of New Mexico, one of the senators who had officiated during the Watergate commission. We also had a noted geologist on board who was a geological professor at a prominent university back in the States.

These guards were taking no chances. Once the passengers were boarded and the aircraft door closed and locked, they returned to the terminal building. Engine start was requested, granted and we were soon airborne to "DAMAS."

Roger was flying, and I was in the right seat handling communications. Upon contacting departure control, I was asked our estimate to the *FIR* (Flight Identification Region).

Not even sure I knew what the FIR was, as I hadn't remembered being asked that en route to Athens, I asked Roger. Pointing to a thin line on the aeronautical chart were lightly written letters *FIR*. Informed that we had indeed been asked our estimate to the FIR on arrival to Greece. I guess I just missed it. Welcome to international flying!

I took a *WAG* (wild ass guess), and thankfully, reached the FIR within the allotted three minutes either side of crossing. Just dumb luck! I had no idea of time constraints to meet this estimate. I just got lucky.

Flying at flight level 410 (41,000 feet) and at approximately 90 miles from Damascus, I requested a lower altitude. Told to *maintain* flight level 410, we were cleared directly to Damascus. This seemed very strange.

I was wondering if the controllers were aware of our destination, as we were told to maintain our altitude. They were very aware. Advised that when cleared for the approach, it was to be commenced from 41,000 feet spiraling down over the top of the airport as nearly as possible until turning on final approach from where a landing could be made.

This had been a common procedure in use for over a year due to Middle East turmoil and was very difficult to execute. We hadn't been made aware of it.

A full-blown factional war was ongoing in Beirut located just the other side of the mountain range separating Lebanon from Syria. Several missile installations were sighted among the mountain ridges. It was only later we discovered they were Russian SAMs. Syria and Russia were allies then as they are now.

Fatigue had long ago settled in. The instrument approach into Damascus was hardly textbook. Upon landing, we were marshaled to the Pan American Airlines ramp for overnight parking; Russians and Russian aircraft everywhere.

Told that fuel purchases had to be requested and made at the airport general manager's office, we located his office in a separate wing of the airline terminal building. It seemed deserted. As I turned to leave, Roger said, "Wait a second. I see someone behind the desk."

There was indeed! A man was kneeling in prayer upon a small rug, intermittently bending at the waist, lost in his morning prayers.

Before I could stop him, Roger walked over and tapped him on the shoulder and said:

"Hey buddy, we need to order some fuel for our Learjet."

The man never stopped praying and Roger, shrugging his shoulders, stepped back and said, "What the hell?"

I said, "Rog, the guy's praying for Christ sake. Leave him be."

"Oh," he said. "I didn't know."

Finally, finishing his prayers, he slowly stood, and while rolling his rug said with a bit of a snarl, in heavily-accented English, "You must be Americans!"

It didn't take a Philadelphia lawyer to figure out the hidden implications of that statement. It was apparent we were not only not well liked but not welcome. Of course, Rogers's behavior did nothing to better this man's opinion of us.

I decided to take a few snapshots of the Russian aircraft crowded on the airline ramp. My little Kodak 110 camera was clicking away when a small military-looking vehicle screeched to a halt in front of me.

A uniformed individual with what I found later to be an AK-47 slung over his shoulder approached yelling a stream of what I presumed was Arabic. He was frantically waving his arms. Snatching the camera from my grasp. Flinging it to the ground and with the butt of his weapon, smashed it to bits. I was stunned, frightened, confused and very unsure what would happen next. Another uniformed individual alighted from the vehicle and in broken English said, "*NO PHOTO!*" I got the message and by the way, welcome to Syria!

Flying Vagabond

44

WHERE THE HELL IS BANGUI?

O ur hotel was located at the airport. The accommodations were adequate. We were both so tired that had they not been, we wouldn't have noticed.

At 8:00 AM my phone rang; it was Aladdin. After a bit of polite small talk, I was told to ready a flight plan to Bangui, Central African Republic.

"Could we possibly leave in two hours?"

I felt like the late Sir Ernest Shackleton blindly exploring the Arctic on that ill-fated voyage years before, praying we weren't about to meet the same fate.

Where Bangui?

A call was made to our Damascus handler, Pan American Airways. Would they please contact Universal Aviation in Houston, advise them of our destination, file our international flight plan, and acquire landing permits for Bangui, Central Africa?

Aircraft fueling commenced, aeronautical charts consulted, flight plan checked, it was discovered Bangui was beyond the range of the Learjet. A technical stop would be required in Khartoum, Sudan. Khartoum was quite a way into Africa, and at the maximum range of the Learjet from Damascus.

Passengers and baggage loaded, the cabin door secured, engines started, we began taxiing for takeoff when the Pan American agent, running, placed himself in front of the aircraft waving his arms for us to stop. It seemed our landing permission in Khartoum, once granted, had now been rescinded. We were going to need to accept a reroute through Egypt with Alexandria as our new technical stop. This would add approximately two to two and a half hours to the trip.

When I mentioned this to Aladdin, he was adamant we should continue to Khartoum.

His reasoning: Khartoum is an Arabic speaking city, and as they, the brothers, were Arabic speakers, there would be no problem. I wasn't sure about this at all. I expressed my concern and told him we didn't know why permission had been rescinded. Perhaps there was some political reason that we were unaware of. He said it didn't matter, that he had been there many times before and that when we approached Khartoum to land, "Pass me the microphone," he said.

He would explain to them, and all would be fine. Young, adventurous, and semi-stupid and with Roger protesting loudly, I agreed and off we went. I may have mentioned earlier that I have a good deal of experience. Unfortunately, as I said earlier, most was from piss poor judgment! This was another of those instances.

Universal, notified by Pan American Airways to reinstate the flight plan to Khartoum, advised that this was not prudent, as they had *not* been made aware as yet of the reason for the landing denial. They did as instructed, however. They advised we were on our own. Hmmmm!

Arriving over Khartoum at flight level 410 several hours later and in a minimal fuel state, we requested permission from Khartoum approach control to land.

Their response was, "Do you have permission to land Khartoum?"

We responded that we had received it once, but it had been rescinded, no doubt because of some mistake. We were now requesting landing permission.

Once again, "Do you have permission to land Khartoum?"

We responded once again that we were now requesting permission to land at Khartoum.

The response we received was rather chilling, to say the least;

"Do not land Khartoum! I say again, *do not land Khartoum!*"

The overhead speakers in the aircraft had been on, and Aladdin, overhearing these transmissions, reached for the microphone.

A very heated, guttural exchange in Arabic took place while we semi-orbited the aircraft at 41,000 feet above Khartoum. After several minutes of this, Aladdin literally threw the microphone in my lap. Crawling to the back of the aircraft, he said, "*Stupid Arabs!*"

Not exactly sure what had just taken place, I mentioned to Aladdin that we were fuel critical and we had to land now. He repeated, "*Stupid Arabs*" instructing me to land the aircraft in Khartoum. He would explain our situation to them when we were on the ground.

"Oh, shit!"

Roger and I exchanged looks. At least 100 silent thoughts passed between us.

We had no choice and declaring an emergency, descended into Khartoum. Once again, we heard; "You do not have permission to land Khartoum. Do not land Khartoum. I say again, *do not land Khartoum!*"

We reiterated that we were an emergency aircraft in a minimal fuel state and we must land. This evoked the same ominous admonition, "*Do Not Land Khartoum!*" I shall never forget that phrase!

Rolling out on final approach, we noticed what appeared to be several military-type armored vehicles aligned on either side of the runway filled with armed soldiers some of whom were aiming their rifles at us.

I immediately yelled for Aladdin to get on the radio as I handed him the microphone. "Please assure these people that we mean them no harm." He immediately did.

Once on the runway and slowing, military vehicles turned onto the runway following as we brought the aircraft to a stop. We were surrounded immediately by armored vehicles filled with frightening looking military personnel all of whom had the weapons trained on us when a tremendous banging on the side of the aircraft door left no doubt they wanted everyone out of the aircraft immediately.

Opening the clamshell doors of the Learjet, Roger was immediately pulled from the aircraft and sprawled on the tarmac. Aladdin and his brothers were frantically screaming in Arabic at the soldiers to not fire their weapons, as we meant them no harm.

A chocolate-colored arm appeared on my right side grabbing and tearing my shirt. With a firm grip on my tie, it proceeded to extricate me from the cockpit.

It was then I noticed an individual alighting from a vehicle that had just arrived on scene.

He was very tall wearing a white flowing robe called a thobe, customary in Sudan. On his head was the ghutrah held on with a black cord of woven goat hair, worn doubled to keep it in place on his head. Shouting orders, all military personnel stepped back allowing him room to approach. Some of the soldiers bowing as he walked by. His English was impeccable with a slight British lilt to it. The bright sun was at his back making it difficult to distinguish his features. My first thought: *Lawrence-of-Arabia lives!*

"Which of you is the captain?" he asked.

Not willing to give that up immediately, I pointed to Roger. He was pointing to me. Lawrence smiled slightly and asked again. "Which of you is the captain?"

I identified myself as the captain. I explained that we were in a fuel critical state and had to land or crash land. Before any further conversation could take place, Aladdin spoke up in Arabic, I'm sure explaining the situation to him in his native language. Introductions ensued, and when Senator Joseph Montoya was introduced, a very marked deference was noticed in Lawrence's voice.

He immediately issued what I presumed to be orders to the surrounding military personnel. The passengers were loaded into what appeared to be an armored personnel carrier and taken to the terminal building. I was instructed to start one engine and taxi the aircraft behind a vehicle that would lead me to parking. I was accompanied by a soldier with a very large gun.

Flying Vagabond

45

WHAT ONE NEEDS IN LIFE ARE THE PESSIMISM OF INTELLIGENCE AND THE OPTIMISM OF WILL

The predicament we found ourselves in was both formidable and challenging. Worrisome would be another way to express it. As one of my passengers was a United States senator, I was optimistic and hopeful for a positive outcome.

Roger and I were soon separated from our passengers; taken to what can only be described as a small, fetid building that at one time must have housed some barn animals. There were no windows, dirt floor, and one bare light bulb hanging from the ceiling. A long bench on one side of the room was the only amenity.

Ushered into this terrible smelling place, we sat on a bench. A soldier with an AK-47 squatted across the room, his gun resting comfortably on his legs. Talking was forbidden. When we tried, this created quite a stir in our little friend with the big gun who was shaking his head in the negative. After what seemed a very long time, the door opened. It was Lawrence. Motioning for me to follow him, I was led to a fenced enclosure several yards from where I had been held. There, behind a chicken wire enclosure, were my passengers. Senator Joe Montoya approached, telling me the American embassy had been notified of our predicament. The American ambassador to Sudan was busy enjoying a quiet sail on one of the nearby lakes. The ambassador's adjutant, however, would soon arrive to solve our dilemma. The senator further informed me that in the early morning hours, Ethiopia had launched an offensive against Sudan. This country was now in a state of war, and we had landed right in the middle of it. It would've been nice to have known that before we took off.

Our hosts, the Sudanese, were very reluctant to allow us to fuel our Learjet. We were trapped! I learned that a Kuwaiti Boeing 707 had just been allowed to land, as it carried a Sudanese government official. I immediately asked if I could board the 707 to speak with the captain. When asked why, I mentioned that I had been told that this type aircraft flying through the Middle East always carried stored fuel in their belly and should they have a defueling hose, it may be possible to extract enough fuel to get us to our destination with a promise of payment later.

Permission was granted!

Boarding the aircraft, I was followed up the boarding steps by an armed Sudanese soldier. The flight attendant at the top of the steps seemed almost apoplectic with fright in seeing this armed soldier coming toward her. I assured her that I just needed to speak with the captain. Would she be so kind as to knock on the cockpit door? The door was opened and the fellow in the left seat, the captain, looked almost exactly like an old British actor by the name of Terry Thomas. He sported an enormous handlebar mustache. This was an all British crew. In very clipped British style, he said, "Allo, is that your Learjet?"

I told him that it was, explaining my predicament, asking if he was carrying any stored fuel.

Turning toward the flight engineer, he asked, "Number two," referring to the flight engineer, "how much-stored fuel are we carrying?"

"Almost 30,000 pounds captain," he replied.

"And have we a defueling hose?"

"No, captain. I'm afraid not."

He responded, "Oh, bad luck that," in typical British fashion.

He then said, "I do have a schedule to keep, old boy," pronouncing the word *shedule* in the British style. "We will keep our ears open for one of your chaps on the frequency and explain that you have yourself 'a spot of bother' over here. Perhaps they might pop in and help you out, but for now, I'm afraid we really must be going. Good luck and cheerio!" I was ushered off the aircraft as the engines were starting.

Exiting the aircraft and looking left, I noticed two barely discernible Boeing 707s that I had not previously noticed. They had American flags painted on their tails and were parked on a distant ramp.

Approaching Lawrence, I asked if I could be driven there to investigate. He approved.

Approaching the aircraft, one of the engine cowlings was opened with a mechanic performing maintenance. An American? It turned out that both aircraft were owned by a former Zantop alumnus of mine, who was staying at the Excelsior hotel in downtown Khartoum. What were the odds?

A telephone was quickly found, greetings exchanged, and within 20 minutes, I was looking at a fellow who I hadn't seen in 20+ years. I remembered him only as Whitey, a nickname and the only name I could remember. He had been a flight engineer on the Argosy and Electra aircraft I had flown. He remembered me. Small world!

Once again explaining my situation, he was more than willing to help. He had a contract between India and Sudan to fly livestock between these two countries. Jet fuel in that part of the world was extremely scarce, and consequently, most large transport aircraft flew around with extra fuel in their bellies. These two were no exception.

The problem, however, was the defueling hose, which no one seemed to have. They really had little use for these hoses, as fuel was just internally transferred from storage tanks to wing tanks and consumed by the engines when needed.

Whitey mentioned the fellow I called Lawrence was called Mohammed, his real name. He would speak to him for me. Mohammed was the Sudanese Minister of Transport. Whitey was sure he could resolve our problem very quickly. Returning to the compound, the American ambassadors adjutant was just arriving. A twenty-something, he was dressed in a fishnet tank top, shorts, and sandals. He informed me that the aircraft would be refueled ASAP and that we should be leaving within the hour. I was quite relieved. During all this time, Roger had been dying from 1000 cuts in this horrible smelling building and entirely and literally in the dark as to what was happening. You can imagine his relief when he was released and told we would be leaving.

I asked Mohammed (Lawrence) if I could taxi the aircraft to a refueling spot or did they have trucks to refuel me. He gestured in the direction of the Learjet. To my horror, several soldiers were pushing on the small wings of this Learjet with two very burly fellows pushing on each aileron; one up, the other down.

I immediately started screaming and yelling while running toward the aircraft with Lawrence following close behind wanting to know what the problem was. I quickly told him, and he yelled at the soldiers to stop. They were pushing it over to a fuel pit for refueling. Talk about a good news/bad news situation. The flight controls could have been irreparably damaged. The controls were quickly checked and, thank goodness, were found to be okay.

Fuel uploaded, passengers boarded, a flight plan filed with the Sudanese authority, a quick goodbye to 'Whitey,' I boarded the aircraft as Lawrence admonished me:

"Do not come back to Khartoum!"

A no-brainer that! A tremendous relief was felt by all once the wheels were in the well.

Flying Vagabond

46

JEAN-BEDEL-BOKASSA

In December 1965, the president of the Central African Republic, David Dacko, was overthrown in a coup. Jean-Bedel-Bokassa was the new president.

The constitution had been suspended, and the national assembly dissolved. In 1972, after seven years in office, Bokassa declared himself *president-for-life* then later in emulation of his hero, Napoleon, appointed himself *Emperor of the Central African Empire* with a coronation ceremony in 1977 costing $20 million U.S. (about $80 million today) practically bankrupting the country. In 1979, he had hundreds of school children arrested for refusing to buy uniforms from a company owned by one of his wives. Bokassa was reported to have personally supervised and taken part in, the massacre of 100 of the schoolchildren by his imperial guard.

I was about to meet this man!

We landed at Bangui M'Poko Airport during a sandstorm. This is referred to as a *simoom* by the locals. There was no local air traffic control radio frequency available at the time. Cairo Radio, several hundreds of miles away, was our point-of-contact for Bangui. Utilizing only HF (high frequency), a radio transmission was initiated announcing our intentions to commence an approach to land at Bangui—a required call.

Cairo acknowledged, advising there were no other aircraft reported in the area.

The only instrument approach to the main runway utilized a primitive non-directional beacon.

It was not very precise, often requiring difficult maneuvering to align the aircraft with the runway centerline as it comes into sight, often only a few hundred feet above the ground. A severe crosswind just added to our misery factor.

The approach and landing, while difficult, went well. Turning clear of the runway, Roger said, "Holy shit!"

I looked over at him. He was looking out of his cockpit window, then suddenly turned to look past me now out of my left window.

A very large, ugly Russian Aeroflot Airlines four-engine transport was braking on the runway, having landed just behind us. We were barely clear of the runway as he shot past. He must have been touching down on the same runway as we were slowing to turn off the runway. So much for, "No other aircraft reported in the area." Had the Aeroflot Aircraft made the required radio announcement, indicating his intention to land at Bangui, we would have let him land first. If it's ugly, it's British; if it's weird, it's French. If it's ugly and weird, it's Russian.

At the very least we could have asked his position and intentions. I soon found that the Russians did pretty much whatever they wanted when flying through these lightly-controlled areas, disregarding convention and regulation. Given the lack of discipline by some foreign carriers, it's a miracle there aren't more accidents in the area.

The reason for our trip to the *dark continent* had not been revealed, but it was obvious that we had been expected.

After parking the aircraft, two older Lincoln limousines drove onto the ramp stopping at the aircraft door. Two very well-dressed drivers and a uniformed individual stood at attention as the passengers alighted the aircraft. Introductions were exchanged; the aircraft was secured.

We were all driven into *town;* Roger and I were dropped at a hotel where reservations had been secured. We were told, "Stay near a phone. You will be called in a few hours."

Several hours later, Aladdin called. A limo would be arriving in about half an hour. "Dress as neatly as possible! We are having dinner with the emperor."

Driven to a beautifully groomed secluded compound, we were greeted by attendants dressed in similar garb as the Vatican Swiss guards. Brightly colored with stripped *pantaloons* (for want of a better word) puffy blouses and knee-length boots.

The *royal palace* was a large but modest-appearing ranch-style home.

Led into a large room, Senator Montoya approached. Across the room stood Aladdin speaking with a distinguished looking individual dressed in a military uniform who wore a gorgeous crimson-colored cape, fringed in white sable fur draped over a heavily bemedaled military uniform.

Could this be *Charlemagne* reincarnated?

No, this was Bokassa, *the emperor!*

Jean-Bedel Bokassa

Surrounding him were several substantial, very black men dressed in dark suits, unsmiling, surveying the room.

Senator Joe approached with a smile asking if we would like to meet his excellency, the Emperor. Feeling a bit stunned by what appeared to be a scene from a long-forgotten movie, I nodded in the affirmative.

The senator advised when introduced, we should bow slightly at the waist. "Do not offer your hand in greeting."

Approaching, it seemed the only thing missing from this man was a crown. One had the distinct feeling of being in the presence of *African royalty.*

"Your Excellency, may I introduce our pilots?" Senator Joe said.

Smiling, the Emperor asked in accented French:

"Are you being seen to? You need but to ask, and your needs will be met."

We thanked him; he turned away, continuing an interrupted conversation. The experience was surreal, to say the least. I asked the senator why we were in the heart of Africa?

He answered, *"Diamonds!"*

This was the reason for the geologist. Explaining further, perhaps tomorrow or the next day, we were to undertake a low-level flight along the length of the Ubangi River as it coursed through the CAE.[20]

The emperor had approved this flight; only the timing needed to be agreed upon. Oh my!

---

[20] CAE was formally known as the Central African Republic (CAR) but now was known as the CAE, the Central African "Empire" as it had been renamed by the "Emperor."

Flying Vagabond

47

TO PUT YOUR LIFE IN DANGER FROM TIME TO TIME...BREEDS A SANENESS IN DEALING WITH DAY-TO-DAY TRIVIALITIES

—Nevil Shute

We had no topographical charts of the CAR/CAE. In fact, we had nothing to indicate where one country ended and the other began. We did know that the Republic of the Congo was to the southwest and the Democratic Republic of the Congo was to the southeast, neither of which were all that friendly. Both country's hated Bokassa.

Two days passed before a time was set. Once airborne, I was to place the geologist in the right seat and, if possible, follow his instructions.

The Ubangi River ran through Bangui and the CAE. Once over the river, I would be asked to descend to approximately one hundred feet or lower and fly as slowly as possible following the course of the river.

We were also to have two of *his excellency's* armed soldiers aboard for security. Their local knowledge would prevent us from entering forbidden airspace.

Once we were airborne and stabilized over the river, Fred, the geologist, replaced the copilot in the right pilot seat.

Coursing slowly, following the bends of the river, at an altitude of one hundred feet, sometimes lower for a better look, I noticed him sporadically marking the topographical map, placing X's along some of the river bank. Wondering why we hadn't been given one of those maps, I asked the meaning of those X's. He replied that he wasn't at liberty to discuss them, finding later that instructions had been given that the guards were for security only and were not to be briefed on the mission. His reluctance spoke to his fear of being overheard.

Airborne for a little over an hour, slow flying the Lear at one hundred feet in what I feared was possible hostile territory was stressful, nerve-racking and had me thinking I needed a good deal of alcohol. Thankfully, we flew only this one trip, as Fred said, "I have seen all I needed." Thank God! Joining the senator later that evening for dinner, I noticed he wasn't looking at all well.

When asked, he said, "I haven't felt well since Khartoum!"

Looking very pale and *drawn*, he adjourned to his room soon after dinner, congratulating me on a good flight. We were to leave in two days hence back to Athens.

48

FORTUNE FAVORS THE BRAVE!

We delayed our departure to late evening, as the temperature was in the 100-degree plus area during the day. The cooler air temperatures would enhance the takeoff performance.

Needing to depart with full fuel tanks, we had filed our flight plan for Heraklion International airport in Crete. This was further than Khartoum had been from Damascus. However, the winds aloft forecast promised a tailwind of more than 100 knots. The flight plans we received indicated we would land with the required fuel reserve.

The flight took us over the Sahara Desert overflying the entire length of the country of Chad and on into Libyan airspace. Looking down on the desert, there were sporadic signs of life that appeared as campfires. These were the fires of the *Bedouins* and the *Touregs*, all semi-nomadic. Volkswagen named one of their SUVs after them. The name Bedouin means *desert dweller* in Arabic. The principal inhabitants of the vast Sahara Desert, however, are the Touregs. The Touregs are a *Berber* people whose desert travels are more often seen in the southwestern part of the Libyan Sahara.

We had been speaking with Cairo on HF (high-frequency radio). Flying at 41,000 feet, the forecasted tailwinds hadn't materialized, and our fuel state was becoming problematic. Benghazi, Libya was about 200 miles distant at our approximate 12 o'clock position. A decision was made to land there for fuel. Easier said than done in this part of the world. A request was forwarded to Cairo Radio seeking permission for a technical stop at Benghazi. A very long time passed when our request was finally granted. We were advised that only U.S. dollars were accepted for fuel—*no credit cards!* Before departing Athens, I had requested $10,000 dollars in cash for contingencies. This was at the advice of Roger who understood better than I, the uncertainties of flying in this part of the world. Cash shouldn't be a problem for us.

We were assigned a VHF (very high-frequency radio frequency). Told to contact Benghazi approach control and then tower frequency, the approach and landing were uneventful. We did not need to execute a spiraling approach as before—a relief!

The fuelers spoke no English. No problem, I had an aircraft full of Arabic speakers. The fueling completed, Aladdin was told that payment was to be made in the control tower to the controller on duty. Aladdin wished to accompany me. I told him there was no need as all tower controllers spoke English albeit accented.

Trudging up the steps of the control tower (no elevator) I was exhausted and could hardly speak when I reached the top. Two men I took to be tower controllers stood staring at me.

They were not smiling! Dressed in traditional Arab garb and despite being air traffic controllers, they had limited English language skills. However, they did understand, *"How much?"*

I was handed a piece of paper upon which was written; **$4000 U.S.** Surely a mistake. I tried to explain that if the aircraft took $800 dollars' worth, I would have been surprised. (Fuel was supposed to be cheap in this part of the world.) They kept pointing emphatically to the piece of paper. Okay, I got it. Jesse James used to live in these parts. The money was in a large envelope in my jacket pocket.

Turning away, as not to let them see how much I was carrying, I counted out $4000. Now they were smiling; I asked for a receipt. Yeah right! I beat a hasty retreat. Arriving at the aircraft, I explained to Aladdin what had just taken place.

Becoming furious, he shouted that he should have accompanied me to the tower. Deplaning the aircraft, he was almost running toward the tower followed closely by two of his brothers yelling and gesturing for him to stop. He did! A conversation ensued, and they all returned to the aircraft. Had he been successful, I fear that it would have gotten very ugly, very quickly. Roger and I may have been once again unwilling guests of a not so friendly people. Another crisis averted!

Flying Vagabond

49

YOU HAVE TO MAKE UP YOUR MIND ABOUT GROWING UP AND BECOMING A PILOT. YOU CAN'T DO BOTH!

L anding in Athens after this African adventure was a relief. Reservations had been made at the Caravel Hotel, one block from the Athenian Royal Palace and King George Square.

We had never been given a timetable of planned flights. We were told, however, that our services would be required for an indeterminate amount of time. Decisions would soon be made regarding future flights. "Please be patient," we were advised.

In the meantime, a tour guide was provided courtesy of Athens Aviation. Her name was Bessie and the secretary to the manager of the facility.

A virtual font of knowledge regarding all manner of Greek and Roman history, she spoke five languages. Her English was every bit as good as mine.

She introduced me to the *Platka,* the old city of Athens. Located in or near the center of Athens, it was an amazing area of wonderful restaurants, bazaars, and shops of all types selling everything from dead animals to shoelaces. Ancient Roman ruins were also in evidence everywhere, especially in this part of

Athens.[21] Many fun-filled days were spent climbing over and around every Roman and Greek ruin we came upon and to think, I was being paid while experiencing great food, great wine, great history and great company. Bessie was 35, beautiful and filled with boundless energy. I was two years older than her and was frequently left gasping trying to keep up with her as we climbed over ancient ruins. I felt like a small child following her everywhere and enjoying every minute of it. The cultural immersion of this historic region is as memorable to me today as she is.

---

[21] The Roman emperor, Hadrian, was a "Philhellene," an admirer of all things Greek. He built the "Arch of Hadrian" the ruins of which can still be seen.

50

SAFETY SECOND IS MY MOTTO

—Ormer Locklear

Receiving a call from Aladdin, I was told to file a flight plan and ready the aircraft. We would be flying to Beirut, Lebanon.

It was during this time in early 1977 that Beirut was in the throes of a civil war, which began in 1975.

All the local television stations were continually broadcasting the horrendous events taking place in Beirut. Aladdin assured me that we shouldn't *worry,* as he and his brothers were originally from Beirut, having moved their business to Athens when fighting broke out there. They assured me they were still politically connected in Lebanese politics, such as it was. Despite the fighting, his business interests in Lebanon had not waned, and indeed were flourishing, he said.

This was the second time he told me *not to worry*. I reminded him that the first time he told me not to worry didn't work out very well.

He stated the barely functioning Lebanese government had granted us permission and *guaranteed* our safe landing as well as safe handling once on the ground. He went on to say they had been alerted he and his brothers would be arriving in a Learjet, explaining to them that it was a small corporate jet painted red and white, registration number *N711AF*. I asked, "Did you also tell them that there was a very large *American Flag* painted on the tail of the aircraft?"

He replied, "No." He would let them know.

Oh, well, okay then!

Beirut's airport, while closed to commercial traffic, was still functional and under the full control of those *friendly* government forces.

Curious, I asked, "Just what did Fadi Shipping ship."

"Oil!" he responded!

Explaining Fadi Shipping's primary business in the Middle East was the transporting of Russian sweet low sulfur oil to the refineries of the Middle East.

At this point in my life, all I really knew of the Middle East was that's where the oil was *FROM!* I found this to be incongruous!

It was explained, Middle Eastern oil was generally of a higher sulfur content and much more difficult to refine. Russian oil, being much lower in sulfur content, was easier to refine, and in higher demand. Despite the civil war raging throughout the city, this form of commerce, while slowed by the fighting, was still ongoing in the northern regions of Lebanon.

I asked, "How did the war start?"

"Various Muslim sects had been fighting each other for thousands of years, interpretive differences of the Koran, being the primary cause," he replied.

To paraphrase him: The fighting ebbs and flows among these sects as their underlying smoldering hatred of one another and of non-believers, ebbs and flows. The war in Lebanon will one day cease. History stands testament. However, that hatred will once again ignite in another part of the world, as common ground is never sought, and common beliefs are even further afield.

This was a sobering prophetic thought, and something we would be wise to remember.

I didn't like any of this and had some very strong reservations. Both Roger and I agreed that it may be one of the foolhardiest things we ever considered doing. The consensus, however, was, "Let's give it a shot." No pun intended!

Flying Vagabond

51

SPEED IS LIFE,
ALTITUDE IS INSURANCE!

We were about to put that to the test!

A glorious Saturday morning welcomed our departure from Athens Ellinikon Airport—now closed.

Blue azure skies, white puffy marshmallow clouds, and a cobalt blue sparkling Aegean/Mediterranean Sea below[22] instilled a mild euphoria lending itself to a greater feeling of happiness, confidence, and pride in this wonderful profession called aviation.

A smooth ride and a following wind soon found us approaching Beirut, Lebanon. We were once again at FL410.[23]

Contacting Beirut approach control, we requested a lower altitude."

"Cleared to Beirut. Maintain FL410 until 20 DME (miles from the airport) then descend to FL300 (flight level 30,000 feet) by the boundary of the Beirut airport and report reaching FL300," came the reply.

From our high-altitude vantage point, we could clearly see Damascus, Syria in the distance on the opposite side of a dividing mountain range.

---

[22] The Aegean Sea is an elongated embayment of the Mediterranean Sea located between Greece and the Anatolian Peninsulas, i.e., between the main lands of Greece and Turkey.
[23] 41,000 feet

Never having been to Beirut before, we found this clearance a bit strange, but nevertheless, we were obliged to follow it. We reported reaching flight level 300 then were advised to fly an orbiting pattern above the airport and to contact Beirut tower. We could see the Damascus airport in Syria. It was that close but divided by that mountain range fringed with SAM missile revetments.

Contacting Beirut tower, we were asked for our permission number to land at Beirut airport.

Complying, we were instructed to begin a spiraling descent to final approach for runway 18. "Report on a five-mile final!" This proved to be a rather dicey maneuver once again, as the winds at higher altitudes were difficult to judge and particularly in a constant-banked descending turn. All those hours spent learning how to fly, doing turns about a point while trying to keep a wingtip over a fixed object on the ground, now proved useful. If only I could have remembered how to do it.

Finally rolling out on a 180-degree heading for runway 18, and reporting 5 miles out, we were cleared to land. We saw columns of black smoke and occasional explosions in the distance as we approached the runway.

Slowing to our final approach speed of approximately 125 knots and 800 feet above the ground, a broken white line arched its way across the front of the aircraft seeming to rise toward us in a slow-motion arc, descending as it passed the nose of the aircraft. This startled the hell out of us. This happened twice in rapid succession. Roger, grabbing the controls of the aircraft shoved the throttles to the stops, diving for the runway.

I asked what was happening and he told me from his experience in Vietnam, those were *tracer* rounds of fire directed toward us. Someone was trying to take us out of the air. We touched down on this 10,600-foot runway at just under approximately 170 knots. If someone was still firing at us, we couldn't tell, as we hoped they were behind us now.

Roger deployed full reverse thrust, pulling up and aft on the reverse thrust levers to their full travel. Both engines responded immediately with a high increase in RPM. The resultant thrust now shook and rocked the aircraft as it was deflected forward slowing the aircraft.

We were both literally *standing* on the wheel brakes at the top of the rudder pedals.

At that moment, several thousand feet down the runway, a vehicle entered the runway with the driver frantically waving for us to follow him.

Driving us into a very large empty aircraft hangar, the doors closed immediately behind us. Securing the engines, I reached to set the parking brake with a trembling hand. Adrenaline levels were high as an involuntary shudder coursed through my body. Not a word passed between us. We just sat dazed, relieved to be safely on the ground.

Our passengers were visibly shaken. Aladdin, advised of the incident, became furious storming off looking to give someone hell.

In discussing his choice to land the aircraft, Roger rationalized the landing stating that a missed approach would more than likely place us once again over *Indian territory*. I thought: So, we instead landed among them! The problem was, we still had to take off at some point. What the hell were we doing there?

Flying Vagabond

52

THE PEARL OF THE MEDITERRANEAN

That is how Beirut had been described before the factional war. It had been at one time, the most beautiful city on the Mediterranean. Beautiful sandy beaches stretching delightfully to calmly breaking waters lapping at the golden sand while in the near distance, majestic snow-capped mountains welcomed skiers from around the world.

The pearl had not only lost its luster; it had all but disappeared. The carnage of war-torn streets and buildings lent testament once again to man's inhumanity to man.

We were in a huge four-wheel-drive vehicle of unknown origin. Our driver was the same person who guided us into the aircraft hangar at the airport.

His name was *Jesus*—pronounced *Hey-soos*. His mother had been Bolivian and his father Lebanese. They had lived in Brooklyn, New York for quite a while where Jesus learned his English.

Emigrating to Lebanon 10 years before, he had since become fluent in Arabic, and he was to be our constant guide and companion. He was also a type A personality, darting this way and that all the while speaking in staccato bursts almost unintelligibly. We were in his charge hoping for the best.

The *Beau Rivage* hotel was in as yet an undamaged part of the city. Various media groups were using this hotel to file their reports of the war. They were quite surprised to see two young Americans being ushered into the lobby. We were suddenly put upon, questioned extensively as to who we were. What were we doing there? How did we get there? How long were we staying? Were we from the American government? Were we military in civilian clothes?

Jesus deflected most of the questions on our behalf explaining in his slightly-accented English and excellent Arabic that we were American business pilots whose businessmen passengers were the guests of the Lebanese government.

This remark brought a stream of more questions as Jesus cleared a path leading to the check-in desk.

With keys in hand, the elevator doors closed leaving reporters and their questions behind. That experience was a brief taste of what celebrities must go through, albeit in a completely different context.

Both of our rooms were threadbare, with many pieces of furniture missing.

We did have beds, but if I hadn't looked, I would've sworn they were made of concrete. The mattress consisted of a plywood sheet covered with several blankets for cushioning and was very hard! Frankly, the room was a wreck having been stripped of almost everything useful. Breakfast the following morning consisted of couscous, tabbouleh, yogurt with some hard-boiled eggs, and hard rolls. We both wondered where the eggs came from, as there didn't seem to be any place left to get them. Evidently, we were now old news, as the few reporters present in the dining room completely ignored us. It was a relief to be sure.

53

AS A PILOT, ONLY TWO THINGS CAN HAPPEN TO YOU. ONE OF THEM WILL!

1. *One day you will walk out to the aircraft, knowing it is your last flight.*

2. *One day you will walk out to the aircraft, NOT knowing it is your last flight!*

Jesus arrived at about 10:00 AM with a message from Aladdin: we were to depart at 1:00 PM for Damascus, Syria. Please make ready!

Jesus was jabbering something about the Syrians crossing into Lebanon during the night and had now set up checkpoints around the airport. He said he had to pass through three checkpoints between the airport and the hotel and for us to be sure we had our passports, pilot's licenses, and any other documentation we may have to assist in getting us through these checkpoints. The Syrian forces were part of a peacekeeping contingent operating under the auspices of the United Nations.

Approaching the first checkpoint on our drive back to the airport, Jesus reminded us to remain calm. He would do all the talking. He asked us to ready our documentation and to do only what he asked of us *when* he asked us.

Rounding a bend in a very rough road, we saw two tanks on either side of the road with a contingent of armed soldiers, perhaps 10 or 12 milling about.

Stopped by two soldiers with AK-47s slung over their shoulders, one on each side of the vehicle peered through the rear windows, which were down due to the heat, demanding identification. Their manner of speech was loud, abrupt, and quite frightening. Speaking rapid-fire, Jesus was explaining who we were in Arabic. The clearest memory I have of this checkpoint was when one of the soldiers nearest me, sticking his head in the window, speaking in Arabic, pointed to my passport. His breath almost brought tears to my eyes. It smelled as though he had just digested a whole goat. Both Roger and I had difficulty just keeping from gagging.

After much conversation between Jesus and the soldiers, our passports and documentation were returned, and we were sent on our way.

The second checkpoint was easier to traverse, as I believe they had been alerted we were coming. However, the third checkpoint nearest the airport still lives in my memory as one of the most traumatic and horrific events I have ever witnessed.

A much larger force of Syrian military vehicles and soldiers, with what I assumed to be Syrian flags flying, were present at this checkpoint, perhaps because of the proximity of the airport. Once again Jesus was speaking rapid-fire to one of the soldiers.

Our passports were again produced. It was during this inspection that a great commotion developed on the opposite side of the road.

Soldiers were shouting, weapons were brandished and fired in the direction of a man running flat out for his life. We didn't know why he was running or what he was running from. He didn't run far. His body exploded in a cloud of pink mist as the force of the bullets propelled his body, coming to rest against a tree covered in blood. Opening his door, Roger threw up, the sight of which evoked a similar and rapid response from me. Jesus yelled for us to pull ourselves back into the vehicle, as we had been cleared through the checkpoint.

Several of the soldiers were laughing, pointing to where we left our breakfast on the road. We were shaken to the core! Roger had seen people killed during his Vietnam days. It still bothered him terribly. Being ex-Navy, I had never seen anyone killed in front of me before. That memory still haunts me!

Arriving at the hangar, our aircraft was under the protection of several armed individuals from the night before. Several Syrian soldiers eyed us suspiciously. They were standing around the aircraft, some leaning on the wings, several more looking through the windows. I don't believe they had ever seen a Learjet before in their lives.

Jesus was once again front and center explaining to what appeared to be the officer in charge that we were the pilots and that we were there to ready the aircraft for a flight to Damascus.

He went on to explain that our passengers would be arriving soon and that I needed to be allowed, as the captain, to proceed to the terminal building where I could file an international flight plan. Permission granted, Roger was left to look after the aircraft as Jesus drove me to the terminal building.

Once inside, I was directed to the third floor where Lebanese air-traffic specialists could assist me in garnering the required international clearances and overflight permits to make such a flight. We had been unable to reach our international flight planning agency, no doubt because of the war. We were on our own! Ever since the checkpoint incident, I had been sick to my stomach and was still charged with adrenaline, my hands shaking noticeably from time to time.

Walking up the stairs, Jesus stopped to talk to someone coming down the stairs. It appeared they knew each other. Continuing, I was two landings ahead of him when I was confronted by a Syrian soldier. Speaking gruffly to me in Arabic, I had no clue what he was saying as I attempted to explain that I did not understand. I pronounced *pilot* 15 different ways trying to get him to understand who I was as I kept walking, smiling the whole time. I did not have a uniform on, which would've helped immensely—that uniform thing again. Dressed only in slacks and a sports jacket, he eyed me suspiciously as I passed. Suddenly, reaching out, he grabbed me by the shoulder spinning me around. I lost my footing, falling backward down several steps coming to rest on my back, paperwork spilling onto the steps.

Pointing his weapon at me, shouting in a frightening manner about who knows what, I too began shouting: "Americano! American! Gringo! Jesus!" I shouted—not hey-soos, *Jesus* then *"HEY-SOOS!"* Hearing the commotion, Jesus came running. Immediately launching into rapid-fire Arabic, he screamed, I assumed explaining who I was and what I was doing there. Asking for my passport, I explained it was in the inside pocket of my sports coat. "Give it to him," Jesus said.

I gasped that I wasn't about to reach into that pocket to retrieve it.

"Tell him where it is and advise him that if he wants it, he can reach down and get it," I said.

Jesus reached instead, handing it to the Syrian.

Upon inspection—I doubt he knew what he was looking at—the soldier threw it upon my still prone body, slung the AK back on his shoulder and stormed off. *Peacekeepers!* Yeah, uh huh!

I told Jesus to never leave me alone again. My blood pressure must have been off the charts, not to mention the bad bruising from falling.

The flight plan and proper clearances were filed and received. We returned to the aircraft. The aircraft had by now been fueled and was sitting on the ramp. Aladdin was carrying on a conversation with a Syrian officer. Noticing my return, he said his goodbyes to the officer and boarded the aircraft. I said my goodbyes to Jesus wishing him well as Roger started the engines.

It was his flight leg, and I was more than happy to let him fly as my adrenaline levels had still not returned too normal. We would still be in *Indian territory* for several minutes after departure. A climb as rapidly as possible to altitude was planned. We had uploaded as little fuel as necessary to get us there with a reserve, thus keeping the Lear as light as possible to expedite the climb.

Clearance was received to taxi to runway 18. Checklists completed, we reached the runway and were cleared for an immediate takeoff. The takeoff was uneventful. Climbing like a homesick angel, the Lear reached FL 410 in record time. No one appeared to be shooting at us this time. I was never so happy to leave anywhere in my entire life.

Beirut to Damascus usually would be an approximately 10 to 15-minute flight. However, because of flight restrictions and those SAM missile sites placed on top of the dividing mountain range, our flight now took us over southern Turkey, where we had overflight permission, entering Syria from the north. The flight time now was 1 hour 30 minutes. I couldn't have cared less. Once at cruise altitude, I immediately slipped into a *coma* allowing my adrenaline levels to stabilize. My eyes didn't relight until Roger woke me approaching Damascus where once again a spiraling approach was made to a landing. We were getting pretty good at that.

54

"QUOD ABSURDUM EST!"
IT IS ABSURD

We were only to be in Damascus four hours, departing for Athens, Greece at 1900. (7:00 PM). Flight plans were filed with Universal Airways and once again, overflight permits requested.

Fueling was handled by Pan American Airways, who had handled all our past flights. They were efficient and somewhat friendly.

Aladdin offered us a ride into the city to visit the famous Damascus bazaar, waiting patiently for us while flight arrangements were made for our return flight to Athens. Unusual! In past arrivals to Damascus, he couldn't wait to leave the airport.

It wasn't long when the reason for his patience became evident.

During the drive into the city, Aladdin asked if we would be willing to be his permanent crew living in Athens. While I enjoyed Athens, the money that he offered for full-time pilot services was less than he was paying us at the time. We both found this to be an absurd proposal. He explained that if we became his employees we would be U.S. tax exempt and that was why the pay *seemed* less. Less is less! No deal! He then asked if I would find and vet two new Learjet pilots to replace us. It just so happened, while on a previous flight to Jeddah, Saudi Arabia, I met two Arab Wings pilots looking for a change of employment: one German, the other Swedish. Arab Wings flew Lear 35s with several bases in the Middle East. Saudi Arabia nationally owned the company. Arab Wings crews required the captains to be well-experienced Learjet pilots. This resulted in most being from Europe, Australia, or the States. All copilots were required to be Middle Eastern, mostly Saudi's. Both captains had given me their contact information, asking that if I heard of anything in terms of Learjet employment would I please call them. I called them.

Both were very interested. Arrangements were made to meet in one weeks' time at the Caravel Hotel in Athens. Traveling together, they both arrived at the Caravel just in time for lunch. Discussion was held, questions answered, i.e., as many as we could.

I expressed Fadi's requirement for two experienced Learjet captains. Being grossly underpaid and overworked at Arab Wings, both were poised to jump ship at the sniff of a better job.

A meeting was arranged at the offices of Fadi Shipping. After introductions to Aladdin and the brothers, both Roger and I were asked to wait in the outer offices while interviews were conducted. Over an hour passed when Aladdin's office door opened with handshakes and smiles all around. Invited into the office, it was announced that both captains had been accepted, accepting Aladdin's offer. They were given a start date in one weeks' time.

Roger and I were advised that first-class commercial flight arrangements were at that time being made for our return to our respective homes stateside. Thanking us profusely for our services, two envelopes containing $1000 U.S. in each, were handed to us—a bonus!

I can't say I was sorry about leaving. The flying had been extremely stressful but at the same time, a great adventure filled with memorable experiences. Almost a year had passed with many trips into Saudi Arabia, Jordon, Syria, and Africa. There would be no more dangerous trips into Beirut.

We were anxious to return home.

Flying Vagabond

55

HOME FIRES

A ll the Jeppesen manuals were boxed up and sent back to "Windstar Aviation" at Westchester County Airport, White Plains New York. I included a note expressing my thanks, volunteering to help with the needed revisions, as they were grossly out of date now. The airway revision charts arrived almost daily in the old days and were quite labor intensive to keep up-to-date. There were no iPads in those days. Thank goodness, I never heard back from them.

Even though we were homeward bound, departing Athens was difficult. Bessie, Athens Aviation secretary, agreed to give us a ride to the airline terminal. She had been our tour guide, our interpreter and all-around *girl Friday* while in Athens. I was going to miss her and Athens. To have the marvelous history of the *birthplace of democracy* explained to me from a very knowledgeable native was an unexpected treat. My memories of Greece will be cherished forever.

Boarding our BOAC [24]Trident jet bound for London, we were surprised to see Senator Joe Montoya seated in the first-class section. He had come and gone several times to Athens in the ensuing months. We never had him as a passenger on the aircraft

---

[24] Now British Airways.

again after the first African trip. As it turned out, my assigned seat was next to the senator's. I don't think this was serendipity.

Our flight arrangements were made by Aladdin's secretary. During the flight to London, Joe did admit to requesting that if possible, we be seated together.

The senator had a Piper Aztec aircraft on his ranch in New Mexico, and he needed a pilot. He expressed his hope that I would accept his offer of employment. He went on to say how much he enjoyed meeting and flying with me, expressing his respect for both my skill and professionalism. I was quite flattered but at the same time, turned him down.

Arriving in London, we all said our goodbyes, each of us on separate flights to our respective homes.

Several months later, I read of Senator Montoya's untimely demise. No cause was given. I have often wondered if his African illness contributed to his death in some way. The senator was a delightful person, a good and honest man, as good and as honest as one can be as a politician.

I had returned home once during my extended European stay for a period of about a week. My marriage had been shaky when I left the first time, made worse when I left the second time. Arriving home now, I found the fire had gone out completely. We both agreed we should make plans to separate. Upon hearing the news, my three daughters collectively wondered what had taken us so long to arrive at this decision. So much for worrying about the kids!

56

EVERY TIME YOU FEEL YOURSELF
BEING PULLED INTO OTHER
PEOPLE'S DRAMA, REPEAT THESE
WORDS: "NOT MY CIRCUS.
NOT MY MONKEYS."

—Polish proverb

nemployed with no immediate prospects in sight, I began networking.

It wasn't long before I received a call asking if I would come to Dallas, Texas for an interview. There was an old Hawker 400 that was begging for a pilot.

My name had been brought up by an old acquaintance. During dinner with his employer, the owner of the Hawker, my old acquaintance mentioned he knew of someone just back from overseas and a good prospect. Stating also that I was type rated in the Hawker and unemployed, he was asked to give me a call.

The company was called *Executive Jet Transport,* which despite its name, was not a jet charter operation. It was corporate owned, the principals of which were Las Vegas casino owners.

The company name was an umbrella under which many smaller companies were operated. It was Dallas-based, as that is where the young chairman of these companies lived and worked.

I was met, driven by limo to what can only be described as a palatial mansion located in Richardson, Texas, the home of the chairman.

"Just call me Jim," he said as we shook hands.

Intelligent and dynamic, I was surprised to learn that during the few days between my receiving the call to come to Dallas and my arrival in Dallas, a rather thorough background check had been made of me.

He knew more about me than I did about myself, and certainly about what I had been doing for the last few years. Somewhat dismayed but impressed, I listened as he made me a very generous offer. I would've been a fool to turn it down. During this non-negotiation, it became evident, he was used to getting his own way.

A start date agreed upon, I began recurrent Hawker Jet training with Flight Safety in Houston.

He mentioned he was the chairman of 52 corporations, all small but quite lucrative. The one he was most proud of and spoke most freely of was called *Snap & Pops.*

Being the size of a large pea, these small bits were wrapped in paper and contained a tiny amount of explosive powder that when thrown to the ground made a large popping sound. Proving to be extremely popular as well as profitable, they sold like hot cakes.

His fireworks factories, located throughout the South mostly in Arkansas, South Carolina, and Mississippi, were in easy reach of the Hawker Jet. I made many late-night trips to several cities in these states. Jim would arrive back at the aircraft with armloads of shopping bags filled mostly with $100-dollar bills. Placed on the divan in the Hawker, many of the bags would fall over unto the floor, during takeoff, spilling their contents. It was not unusual to find a few bills under the seats when cleaning the aircraft. The first time this happened, I called Jim.

He asked, "How many did you find?"

"Three, I replied!"

"Keep 'em as a gift."

What a guy. It wasn't long before I suspected something was just a little off. Did I mention that Las Vegas casino owners owned these companies? Casino owners, bags full of money, midnight trips! Hmmmm!

"Not my circus. Not my monkeys."

Flying Vagabond

57

IN FLYING AND IN BUSINESS, I HAVE LEARNED THAT CARELESSNESS AND OVERCONFIDENCE ARE USUALLY FAR MORE DANGEROUS THAN DELIBERATELY ACCEPTED RISKS

—Wilbur Wright, (paraphrase) Sept. 1900

The *money trips* as I referred to them, were generally conducted on Mondays, Wednesdays, and Fridays. Most weekends were spent in Las Vegas where Jim conferred with the owners.

These trips for the crew were all expenses paid. The Tropicana, Flamingo, Caesars, The Aladdin, MGM, Riviera, The Dunes, The Jockey Club were just some of the hotels where we stayed. Jim was a gracious host. Everything was 'comped' for us: high-end meals, the top shows; Sinatra, Sammy, Dean, Wayne Newton; anyone we wanted to see.

My very first trip to Vegas with Jim was quite a surprise. Our accommodation was The Jockey Club. A sizable two-bedroom suite had been reserved for us. Opening the door to our suite, there stood three beautiful young ladies smiling like Cheshire cats. Fearing that I had entered the wrong room, I apologized and checked the room number and key; I was in the correct room. They were in the wrong room...or were they?

They stood giggling, explaining that Jim had sent them to welcome us to Vegas on our first trip with him to *Sin City*.

I instantly upped my respect and regard for him and just as quickly demonstrated my gratitude to these fine young ladies who took so much of their time and effort to welcome us. I wasn't sure if I was going to be arrested working for this guy, but I was sure that until then, I wasn't going to worry about it!

One such weekend trip, I was the guest of one of my former Rock-n-Roll groups, *The Three Dog Night*. They had a gig at the MGM Grand. Treated to backstage privileges, I was invited to their after-show party in the same hotel.

Memories of decadence and debauchery that would have made Caligula proud came flooding back.

I was delighted to have been invited. I sometimes think that I should be in a jar, on a shelf in some science lab somewhere. I don't know how I survived those parties.

Just to be clear, while drugs were readily available, I *NEVER* indulged in that activity. Frankly, I just didn't then and still do not now understand the fascination.

Several months passed. The routine gradually became boring.

The restaurants, the shows were all great, but we rarely spent much time in Dallas. My wife and I had separated again but not divorced. I found a very lovely young lady in Dallas and was growing quite fond of her but my being away a good bit began to strain that relationship. I started to think of perusing other opportunities, both marital and employment-wise.

I didn't have long to wait. It was the middle of the week when Jim called and said:

"Fuel up the Hawker! We are leaving for Vegas ASAP."

This was unusual. We always had plenty of warning in the past of such trips. Arriving at the Dallas Love Field, a fuel truck had been placed in front of the aircraft.

I hadn't called ahead for fuel so was a bit curious; perhaps Jim had alerted them to our immediate departure, and they were standing by.

Entering the FBO (fixed base operation), I was informed that the last two fuelings had not been settled. Jim had previously been notified by the fueling manager his credit card had been declined. Always promising to make good went only so far. The FBO pulled the plug on future fuelings until arrears were settled. Unsettled, the fuel truck blocked the aircraft from moving.

Reaching Jim as he was leaving his home, I explained the situation. He advised he would take care of it when he arrived. He did, in cash!

While en route, Jim explained that there had been a misunderstanding of sorts regarding finances in Vegas and that he would be about two hours.

"Stay with aircraft," he ordered.

A misunderstanding of finances sounded ominous. This was Vegas, and these were very serious people he was in bed with.

I never saw him again!

Flying Vagabond

58

FOR MAXIMUM ATTENTION, NOTHING BEATS A GOOD MISTAKE!

everal hours had passed, when a three-car limo entourage arrived at the door of the aircraft. Assuming this was Jim arriving with guests, I instructed the first officer to immediately activate our instrument flight plan to Dallas and to request an airway clearance.

As the first limo arrived, the front passenger door opened and the largest man I had ever seen slowly unfolded himself from the front seat.

Walking toward the limo, I expected Jim to exit the back door at any moment. As I approached the limo, this tremendous individual, whose arms were gorilla length attached to hands the size of hams, pushed roughly against my chest while asking;

"Where the fuck are you going?"

Shocked and off-balance, I explained that I was the pilot of Jim's aircraft and thought he might be in the limo. The *gorilla* looked at me saying, "Jim ain't comin'!"

While this exchange was taking place, an impeccably dressed older man, exited the limo and, in a very soft-spoken voice, addressed the larger man, asking him to step aside. Smiling as he approached and with hand extended, he introduced himself as a business partner of Jim's.

I was to discover, he was also the sole owner of the Aladdin hotel among other things. [25] Mentioning that Jim would not be accompanying us on this flight to Dallas, he introduced me to his look-alike son and three other associates. There was no mistaking, who was in charge. We boarded the aircraft for our flight to Dallas Love Field.

"Captain, when airborne and you feel you can leave the cockpit, would you please come back, as there are many things we need to discuss."

At this point, I didn't know what to think. Where was Jim and why wasn't he on board? Was he dead, was he alive, was he being held against his will?

I had long thought that by working for this fellow, Jim, I may inadvertently and unknowingly become illegally involved in some underhanded activities. Those midnight runs through the South, shopping bags full of money and the extravagant way Jim threw money around, a case in point.

Most of us have wisdom that enables us to recognize an undesirable old acquaintance: *the folly that we have already embraced.* This wisdom of recognition often manifests as one's inner voice of warning, an inner voice whose message intruded on my psyche several weeks before.

Upon reaching altitude and on autopilot, my first officer took over flight deck duties.

As I entered the cabin, taking a seat, a round of questioning began, some of a personal nature and several more regarding the activities of Jim and our past flight operations.

---

[25] It was only later that I discovered that this mild-mannered, soft-spoken, impeccably-dressed little man was often referred to as the godfather of the Lebanese mafia by some of his associates.

How long have you been working for Jim? Are you married? How many children? Are you from Dallas? Do you have an apartment in Dallas, or do you own a home? Would you be interested in a move to Las Vegas? How many pilots did Jim employ? Are there any other aircraft? How many flights a week did we make through the South? Did we ever see or notice bags of money being brought aboard the aircraft? Was the aircraft ever used for Jim's personal flights?

Each question was becoming more ominous than the one preceding it.

Told that Jim was no longer a part of the organization, he explained we no longer were working for him. He said that Jim made several gross errors and mistakes and had been deposed as chairman and fired from the mother corporation. This was probably going to be the last flight on this aircraft. The aircraft had been on lease. I was informed the lease had been canceled and paid off that day. "The lessor's pilots would be picking up the aircraft in Dallas in a couple of days," he said.

Would I please notify all other employees connected with the aircraft; pilots, mechanics, etc. of what I had just learned, and would all involved please meet at Jim's office at the Honeywell center on Mockingbird Lane in Dallas at 8:00 AM the following morning no doubt, a resume generating meeting.

Well, I had been looking for a job a year ago when I found this one. This was getting old!

Flying Vagabond

59

THE MAIN THING IS TO TAKE CARE OF THE MAIN THING

Executive Jet Transport had three aircraft, four pilots, and one maintenance technician. The aircraft consisted of one Hawker Jet model 400, a leased Learjet 24 and one Piper Seneca II—also on lease. The Hawker was the primary aircraft used exclusively by Jim.

The Learjet was used to fly Jim's wife and company sales executives on occasion. The Seneca was primarily used for short hops around Texas. It was all about to end.

I had been considering looking for other employment, but I wasn't quite ready to join the ranks of the unemployed just yet. It is easier and certainly better to look for a job while you have a job.

I had been fortunate to find employment so soon after returning from Europe thanks to a friend dropping my name at a propitious moment, but I had been gone from the States quite a long while. Out of sight, out of mind. I felt I had to quickly reestablish my presence among my network of friends.

The meeting commenced promptly at 8:00 AM. Sitting at the end of a very large conference table was Jim's proclaimed business partner. To his right were his look-alike son and the associates I had met previously.

There were two additional people at the meeting, one of which I recognized immediately. His name was Chris Karamanos. Some weeks before, I had been invited to join Jim and guests for dinner at the Dunes Hotel. Chris Karamanos had been one of the guests. Karamanos was a very familiar face in Las Vegas, having run for various political offices in Clark County.

He held a controlling interest in the Thunderbird Hotel and was the owner of T. K. Christy's restaurant, a rather high-end restaurant just off the strip. He also owned a profitable catering business run from the kitchens of that restaurant. He was past vice-president of the Las Vegas Hilton. It was rumored he was well-connected and everything that term implied. He was reportedly a friend of Tony *The Ant* Spilotro of the Kansas City Mafia family who had been found guilty of running a skimming fraud in Las Vegas. In June 1986, *The Ant* was found dead in an Indiana cornfield. I wonder how that happened.

In 1989, Chris himself would be found dead in a Mesquite, Nevada hotel room of a drug overdose. It was ruled a suicide. Ha!

This room was indeed filled with some dangerous people.

The other gentleman was introduced as president of Jet Avia Corporation, a jet charter corporation operating a fleet of Learjet aircraft of which Karamanos was a controlling partner. All of us were immediately offered jobs with Jet Avia.

However, it would be necessary to relocate to Las Vegas at our own expense. The offer, while appreciated, was rejected by everyone.

I did ask what had become of Jim. I was told that this was not my concern. He did mention that Jim was obviously still in Las Vegas and was being *interviewed.* Say no more!

We were asked to gather any personal belongings from all the aircraft. We received one month's severance pay and a handshake and were told the Jet Avia offer would remain open. Just call if we changed our minds.

Jet Avia was the company that on January 6, 1977, lost a Learjet 24, which crashed into a 10,000-foot ridge in the eastern portion of the San Gorgonio Wilderness with Dolly Sinatra on board—Frank's mother. Grief-stricken, Frank vowed to run the company out of business. He did!

The main thing was to take care of the main thing and find another flying job.

Flying Vagabond

60

SUCCESS IS THE ABILITY TO GO FROM ONE FAILURE TO ANOTHER WITH NO LOSS OF ENTHUSIASM

—Winston Churchill

After removing my personal belongings from the Hawker and the Learjet, I informed the manager of the fixed base operation what had occurred. I asked if I could use one of their IBM Selectric typewriters to prepare a resume. There were no computers in those days. He agreed. Overhearing the conversation, one of the ladies at the front desk asked if I was looking for another Hawker Jet flying job. She mentioned that an Indiana-based company, shopping mall developers, had been looking for a qualified Hawker Jet pilot for some time. She stated the chief pilot had asked her if she knew of anyone. Supplying me with the chief pilot's name and home phone number, I immediately called. There was no answer at the office. Calling the home number, a woman answered. Introducing myself, I explained why I was calling. She asked where I was calling from. Mentioning I was currently at Dallas Love Airport, she informed me her husband should be landing at Dallas Love at any minute if not already. She stated he was flying a Hawker Jet 400 model, which was red, white and blue.

Facing the active runway, I saw a red, white and blue Hawker 400 in a landing flare.

"What's the tail number?" I asked.

N61MS!

Bingo!

I watched as the Hawker taxied onto the ramp. The noise from its Viper engines made all normal conversation next to impossible. As the engines were shut down, I approached the aircraft.

Deplaning, I introduced myself to the pilots asking if one of them was the chief pilot. The one I had assumed to be the chief pilot said facetiously, "You don't look like the FBI."

Smiling and assuring him I wasn't, I mentioned speaking to his wife just moments earlier. As might be expected, I had his instant attention, explaining I called looking for him.

"What can I do for you?" he asked.

"I had recently heard of your company's need of a Hawker 400 pilot," I said. Could you spare me a moment of your time?"

He agreed and entering the FBO. We were shown to the conference room.

Presenting my resume, I explained I was current in the Hawker Jet 400 with several hundreds of hours as pilot-in-command in the aircraft.

An hour later, I was invited to dinner and was re-introduced to his first officer. Dinner, drinks, and more questions were asked and answered.

Background of the company, the flight department, its history, mission statement, and long-term goals were explained and outlined. "Should you be successful and brought on board, you would be pilot number six to join the Aviation Department."

Addressing my past chief pilot experience, he asked if I would be comfortable being just a pilot in a large flight department.

I assured him that would not be a problem. Throughout this time, it was clear that I was being carefully observed. He seemed to be paying attention to his first officer's reactions to me.

As the dinner ended, he explained that before an offer could be made, he wanted me to meet *Bill,* explaining that he was his right-hand man and that most decisions regarding new hires would be joint. In two days' time, he would return to Dallas Love Airport bringing Bill with him. The company was opening a new mall in Dallas.

I had been hoping for long-term employment, and so far, it sure sounded good.

61

TO STRIVE, TO SEEK, TO FIND AND NOT TO YIELD!

—Alfred Lord Tennyson

A nasty case of nerves fueled by excitement, apprehension, and adrenaline were all standing tall at my first meeting with Bill. He was gracious and polite and was a Mississippi native with a wonderful Southern accent. Tuning into the cadence of the Deep South, I found him to a warm and friendly fellow. Several days after this meeting, I was provided an airline ticket to Indianapolis, IN; corporate headquarters.

Introduced to the company president, Mr. Gerald Kraft, I was interviewed extensively. The interview was proceeding quite favorably until he asked about my wife and family. I mentioned that my wife and I had separated.

He asked, "Any chance your marriage could be saved?"

I found this rather strange until he mentioned that he equated a sound stable marriage and a happy family life to a sound, stable and happy pilot.

Obviously, he didn't know what the hell he was talking about. He said that this may be a prerequisite to employment. Oh God!

I gave assurances that I would try to affect a positive outcome on the marriage front.

After many days of raised voices and soft discussion with the estranged Mrs., it was agreed we would reconcile.

Mr. Kraft accepted the news with an immediate offer of employment. You may be wondering if the marriage lasted. Yes, an additional five years. [26]

I wasn't immediately accepted by all departmental pilots. Being hired as a captain, one pilot was extremely bitter, feeling he should have been promoted from within the ranks. Serving as my first officer on several trips as his trip captain proved problematic. Obstinance, resentment, non-verbal communication, and ill will filled the cockpit.

I explained I had little to do with the company's decision to pass him over for the left seat; *would he please direct his resentment and frustration elsewhere and get on with the job at hand!* Eventually, he did, and we became good friends.

---

[26] The divorce was not amicable. Contentious and fraught with stress, she was left bitter while I was left bitter and *broke.*

62

"LET ME SHOW YOU HOW IT'S DONE." AKIN TO THE OLD AVIATION SAYING: "I'VE GOT IT"

H ired to captain the Hawker 400, I was informed I would need to fly with the chief pilot until he deemed me ready to be assigned trips as captain. Taking it in stride, I hoped to learn from it. Did I ever! I learned that if I survived, it would be fortunate indeed.

He seemed hell-bent to disprove many laws of physics, aerodynamics, rational and common sense set down by God and the FAA. In short, he scared the hell outta me!

On one such trip into Aspen, Colorado, at best, a most challenging mountain airport, I was relegated to right seat duties as his copilot. I was experienced with the challenges Aspen presented. Several times in the past, I had landed there during my brief sojourn with the Pepsi people.

Aspen airport is almost 8000 feet above sea level and requires a deft hand at the controls, sound judgment, diligent focus, and a basic knowledge of high-altitude aerodynamics.

What I witnessed was a ham-fisted hand on the controls, skewed focus, a marked lack of sound judgment and complete ignorance of high-altitude mountain flying.

Lying in a deep valley, a landing at Aspen requires configuring the aircraft very early, slowing the aircraft and beginning a prompt descent upon clearing *close in* terrain. Airspeed and descent rates must be managed precisely. This approach is daunting and can be very dangerous if executed improperly.

In following years, a new, and somewhat less challenging but no less dangerous instrument approach has been commissioned. Several fatalities through the years stand as silent testimony to the challenges of this mountain retreat airport.

Airspeed control is primary. A high *indicated* airspeed will result in an even higher [27]*true* airspeed due to several factors such as density altitude.[28] The true airspeed rise is approximately 2% per 1000 feet. Thus, an indicated airspeed of 130 knots on final approach into an airport such as Aspen will result in an approximate *true* airspeed of perhaps 20 knots higher.

The runway has a 2% uphill slope on the landing runway, which at the time was only 7000 feet long.

He stated that he was an old hand at Aspen. "Let me show you how it's done," he said.

Being somewhat familiar with the expression, I was on high alert. *I needed to be!*

Failing to configure the aircraft with flaps and landing gear extended to slow the aircraft allowing for a slow airspeed descent into the valley; he pushed the nose over in a dive for the runway.

---

[27] The state of an amount of gas (air) is determined by its pressure, volume, and temperature. The modern form of the equation relates these simply in two main forms as relates to aviation: indicated airspeed and true airspeed.

[28] Density altitude is air density given as a height above mean sea level. Density altitude can also be the pressure altitude adjusted for non-standard temperature.

The airspeed quickly increased beyond the maximum speed to lower the flaps and gear. The runway was in sight and growing larger by the second.

I called out the airspeed expressing my concern we were too fast and clean (no drag devices extended) and needed to pull the nose up drastically to induce drag, slow the aircraft, lower flaps, and landing gear. I grabbed the control column gently, pulling the nose up. He resisted, saying:

"I got it!"

In aviation parlance, this usually means, "I really fucked this up."

Here I was the FNG (fucking new guy) gently attempting to override the controls from the boss. Oh shit!

I said, "Go around. It isn't going to work."

I pulled harder. Speed dropped to maximum landing gear lowering speed. I was pulling; he was pushing. He called for *gear down!*

The landing gear was lowered followed quickly by lowering all the flaps to full landing configuration, slightly over-speeding them. We desperately needed to slow down.

Now too low for a safe *go-around* due to rapidly rising terrain on the far end of the runway, and now in full landing configuration, we were committed: still hot; still high! Forcing the nose over into an ever-higher rate of descent, the airbrakes were deployed. Airbrakes extended while airborne with flaps extended is expressly forbidden in the Hawker Jet. It is a definite danger at any time due to high drag forces increasing descent rates rapidly.

Someone once said, "Aerobatics is like having sex in a car wreck."

Yup! I believe it now. I had never experienced *aerobatics* on final approach before and never in a jet aircraft. A ham-fisted control grip, fueled with adrenaline, pumping of the controls in ever-changing pitch and yaw while careening relentlessly toward perdition, changed all that.

Spectators at an airshow expect to see a spectacle. If anyone had witnessed this display from the surrounding mountaintops, they would not have been disappointed. They should have witnessed it from my seat!

Speed brakes, full landing flap, and a very high descent rate culminated in a very hard, high-speed landing, bouncing and bounding halfway down the runway. Maximum braking was applied. The aircraft was not equipped with thrust reversers. I would have given anything to have them at that moment. Using every inch of the remaining runway to stop the aircraft, I just lost it.

"What the fuck was that? Are you fuckin crazy?" I said.

"It's a wonder the landing gear didn't collapse we hit so fuckin hard! Holy shit that was close. What the fuck were you trying to prove?" I was wondering the whole time what the hell had I gotten myself into?

The jerk had a blank look on his face except for a slight *twitch* of his right cheek. I was to see that *twitch* many more times in my days of flying with this guy. It appeared to be a stress twitch. Admitting he got a *little behind* the aircraft on approach, he explained, he felt he needed the speed brakes extended to help slow the aircraft. Then he added, "It worked out okay."

Yup, except for "Mr. Toads Wild Ride" on final approach and the crash landing; it worked out well!

Overhearing the exchange, the CEO raced forward. He was never one to hold back. "What the fuck was that?" he demanded. "Why was I thrown about the cabin? I goddamned near slid off my seat on landing. Who the fuck landed this thing?" while looking at me.

The jerk's *twitch*, increasing in intensity, stated Aspen approach dropped us too quickly into the valley to the point we were committed to land. He went on with this lie to say that he intended to give them a piece of his mind very soon. What a crock!

The CEO, looking a bit skeptical, seemed to buy into this lie, saying, "See that you do. I had never experienced such a landing here at Aspen before. By the way, where's Bill?" The implication was clear. Had Bill been in the cockpit, this wouldn't have happened.

Not only did he prove himself an incompetent pilot, it seemed he was a liar and a coward as well. It was a very long time coming before I gained the complete trust of the CEO due to this episode.

I had made an enemy of the chief pilot, but I was alive—not a good way to start a new job.

Flying Vagabond

63

THOSE WHO CANNOT REMEMBER THE PAST, ARE CONDEMNED TO REPEAT IT!

—*Jorge Santayana*

Remaining in Aspen for three days, I spent most of the time in my hotel room. I went to dinner with him only once during this period for fear of shortening my brief tenure even more. I was fearful of having to discuss and relive that incredibly unsafe approach and landing. Thankfully, it never came up.

Several days passed. It was summer in the Rockies. On the day of our departure, it was 30 degrees Celsius (86 degrees Fahrenheit). With passengers and several pounds of baggage, we required a fuel stop en route to the Midwest.

I was informed that this flight leg was to be mine. He asked that I calculate how much fuel we could safely carry for our departure from this very challenging airport.

I calculated close to 4000 pounds of fuel. It was just enough to comply with a marginally safe gradient of climb should an engine fail on takeoff—a horrible thought.

He added an additional 1000 pounds of fuel behind my back. WTF!

I had selected Arapahoe Airport, now called Centennial, for a fuel stop. Overriding my decision, he said we were landing at Salina, Kansas a considerable distance away. The takeoff data for our weight were in the *shaded* area of calculations. This indicated that we needed to reconsider our takeoff options.

Should the worst happen, an engine failure during takeoff would probably result in all being killed. Explaining that I felt we were now over gross weight for this takeoff didn't faze him in the least.

Eventually, he agreed that Salina may be a bit of an overreach and he agreed to land at Pueblo, Colorado. Still further than safe! Aspen airport did not have defueling capability at the time. I was stuck with an aircraft overweight condition, an overbearing captain, an overreach in refueling airport choice, and an overactive nervous system. Hope against hope, I mentioned the only thing that could accommodate a safe takeoff now was to delay our takeoff until the temperature cooled significantly. Probably winter!

He replied, "Bullshit! We're going!"

Passengers and baggage loaded, we began our taxi for takeoff. It was a slight uphill taxi to the departure end of the runway, requiring more than normal engine thrust just to get the aircraft moving uphill. It was an ominous and scary sign of things to come.

During the takeoff roll, I felt him on the controls with me.

He was applying slight back pressure on the elevator controls as the aircraft accelerated slowly, thus raising the nose slightly before the aircraft reached flying speed.

He pulled. I pushed! What was wrong with this guy? Raising the nose even slightly during takeoff roll will induce drag slowing the aircraft requiring more runway to become safely airborne.[29]

Our takeoff roll was long, our acceleration rate, very slow. Aspen Airports MSL (mean sea level) elevation is 7815 feet. Density altitude for this day was 13,100 feet. The aircraft became airborne just before the very end of the runway!

Well, now I had seen both ends of the runway. I had used every inch of that 7000-foot[30] runway in both directions. That just isn't supposed to happen. Clearly, an engine failure during rotation would have proved fatal!

---

[29] It had been shown with early wind tunnel tests by De Havilland, the original builder of the Hawker, that approximately 2,500 pounds of drag was induced with a slow, proper takeoff rotation. A catastrophic engine failure during takeoff rotation is a major life-threatening event.
[30] The runway at Aspen has now been extended to 8000 feet.

Flying Vagabond

64

I WANT TO DIE LIKE MY GRANDFATHER, PEACEFULLY IN HIS SLEEP, NOT SCREAMING IN TERROR

Landing at Pueblo, Colorado, the temperature was 100 degrees Fahrenheit. Pueblo is located in the high plains (100 miles) east of Denver.

I ordered a fuel load that would safely get us off the ground with an hour's fuel in reserve on our arrival at Indianapolis. Indy's weather was reported as clear, visibility unlimited, with a warm front between us.

He had been in the FBO (fixed base operation) during fueling.

Seeing the fuelers winding the fuel hoses into the fuel truck, there was no single point fueling on this old Hawker.

He asked, "How much fuel did you put on?"

I said, "Six hundred gallons—4000 pounds." It was enough to get there and about an hour plus extra and very close to the safe limit for takeoff.

He turned to the fueler who had been waiting for me to check the load and said, "Top the wings!" (filling the wings to the maximum). That added 3000 plus additional pounds to an already very heavy aircraft. I literally yelled that this would put us over maximum takeoff weight again, this time by several thousand pounds.

I said, "I can't even calculate takeoff numbers for such an aircraft weight. Temperature, field elevation, density altitude, aircraft weight, and runway length were all either too high or too short!"

Maximum takeoff weight for this aircraft was 23,300 pounds. That was on a standard day of 59 degrees Fahrenheit and at sea level.

Given the ambient conditions and field elevation, we were already several thousand pounds over maximum allowable takeoff weight.

The *twitch* started in earnest, developed into a flutter, culminating in a quiver that seemed to cause his right eye to blink incessantly. The fueler, who had been standing by witnessing this exchange, asked, "Did you say top the wings?"

In a very abrupt and rude manner, he repeated, "Top off the wings!"

I needed a job, but at this point, I wasn't sure I needed *this* job. I didn't think he would fire me, as we were in Pueblo, Colorado. So, I said, "Look at the data!"

I attempted to show him that we had no takeoff numbers for this impending takeoff, not even shaded area numbers indicating a somewhat nebulous area to be calculating takeoff numbers.

He just walked away. I should have done the same. I don't know why I didn't. Hindsight is always 20/20!

The east/west runway at Pueblo, Colorado was precisely 10,000 foot long. That sounds like a lot. However, on this day it was several thousand feet too short to accommodate a *safe*, nay, any takeoff in this aircraft at this weight.

This was unbelievable! Anxious and apprehensive, I kept studying the available takeoff data in the hope of finding some way to convince him to delay this insane takeoff, at the very least to rethink the added fuel.

Refusing to discuss the subject anymore, he said, "Still your leg!" You need to learn how to fly under these conditions."

"WTF! Was this wartime? Mamma Mia," I exclaimed, which sounds a lot better than *"I want my Momma"* from a grown man.

Turning onto the runway, we were cleared for takeoff. Shimmering waves of heat danced above the runway, as I released the brakes and advanced the power levers to full power.

Sun glare and heat waves obscured the departure end of the runway. The aircraft inched forward slowly struggling greatly to accelerate while visions of impending doom clouded my mind.

Density altitude had been too scary to calculate but I was sure it was in the thousands of feet; the ambient air too thin to rapidly propel the engines to required takeoff power. I said a silent prayer.

Pushing forward on the control yoke, I pinned the nose firmly on the runway. The aircraft accelerated slowly through 100 knots, roughly 30 knots below takeoff speed.

Suddenly, "No. No. No. You have to get it light!" he yelled.

Grabbing the controls, the jerk raised the nose of the aircraft off the ground, thereby dramatically and significantly increasing the drag rise, slowing acceleration and increasing the already exceeded takeoff run requirements.

I wasn't aware of speed, as the end of the runway was only a few hundred feet in front of us. I pulled back hard on the controls, getting us airborne as the end of the runway disappeared below the aircraft. The aircraft stick shaker, the warning of an impending stall, sounding almost immediately.

I swear I felt the aircraft drop slightly as the pavement ended. The aircraft had been rotated below safe rotation speed.

Only a few feet off the ground with nothing in front of us but desert, the aircraft, not quite at flying speed, and in ground effect[31] was barely staying in the air. lowering the nose to gain airspeed and thus get the wings flying, I felt the control column being pushed then pulled in a pumping fashion.

The idiot had grabbed the controls on his side of the cockpit and was *pumping* the elevator controls. Continuing this aberrant maneuver, I felt would undoubtedly not end well.

I screamed, "Let go of the fucking controls!" He did!

The control tower asked if we were okay saying they lost sight of us in the dust cloud.

I had heard military pilots refer to this situation as a *pipe dance*. The *pipe*, of course, referring to the tailpipe of their fighter aircraft as it too struggled to gain flying speed with the aircraft nose raised, thus pumping thousands of pounds of thrust of engine power into the earth to escape the surly bonds of earth. About engine power: a lot is good, more is better, and too much is just enough. We had neither. No. This was more like the crippled *Titanic* attempting to stay afloat in a sea of air.

Gently pushing forward on the controls, lowering the nose slightly, the aircraft just a few feet above the ground when V2 speed[32] was reached, a very slow climb was established, mostly by sheer will. We were a considerable distance from the departing runway over amber fields of grain but at last, accelerating slightly. Death was certainly on my mind—not mine, his. I wanted to strangle the bastard! Imperative, immediate, and instinctive, a steely focus had been required to affect a positive outcome of the potential killer of a takeoff. What I didn't need was an asshole in the other seat pumping the fucking controls.

---

[31] Ground effect is the increased lift and decreased aerodynamic drag of a wing close to a fixed surface.
[32] V 2 = Minimum safe climb speed.

Had an engine failed or any obstacle taller than about 10 feet off the runway end and this literally would have been written by a *ghostwriter.*

Much too heavy to reach our filled altitude of 37,000 feet, which had been filed by the *twitch,* we eventually settled for 31,000 feet as a final cruise altitude. Unfortunately, a warm front was between us and destination. As we drew closer, he asked the radar controller for a higher altitude. I stated that I thought we might be too heavy to safely climb much higher.

Receiving clearance and ignoring me, he pushed the throttles up to full power and took control of the aircraft. We were assigned flight level 370 (37,000 feet). Passing through 34,000 feet, the airspeed had slowed to Mach .64, much too slow, and was slowing further.[33]

The heavy weight of the aircraft, as well as abnormally higher temperatures at altitude, precluded us climbing any higher. I asked the controller if we could maintain FL330.

The assholes cheek was now in *full quiver.* He quickly realized that FL330 was the best we could do. He put the aircraft in a slow descent to FL330. A very rough ride ensued. It wasn't long before the chairman asked why we didn't climb. He once again dazzled the boss with bullshit, saying, "We had to take a bit more fuel to make it nonstop to Indy. Otherwise, we would have had to stop at an airport under this weather, and that would have been worse!"

Was there no end?

---

[33] Mach 1.0 is the speed of sound. Mach .64 is 64% of the speed of sound. At this speed, and altitude, we were barely climbing. Much slower and we would be approaching a full wing stall where the aircraft wing could no longer sustain lift.

Flying Vagabond

65

LEARNING A LITTLE BIT ABOUT FLYING IS LIKE LEADING A TIGER BY THE TAIL—THE END DOES NOT JUSTIFY HIS MEANS

But for the rough ride, the rest of the flight proved uneventful. Thank God! Not a word was passed between us except for required cockpit duties. I was sure that I was on my last flight with this company, confident I was to be fired upon landing. I had made up my mind that if I had to continue to fly with this maniac, I should seek employment elsewhere.

The landing was normal. Engines were secured. The aircraft door was opened. We assisted the passengers with their luggage, and he departed the premises without a word to me. Thinking a phone call later that evening would be the death knell of this job, I decided I needed a drink!

Several hours later, while reliving the flight nightmare with my wife, the phone rang.

It wasn't the chief pilot but his number two man, Bill, asking how the flight went. I asked if he had heard from the chief? He replied that he hadn't. Asking why, I told him that I was thinking of quitting.

I told him in detail what had transpired. When I finished, there was nothing but silence on the other end of the line.

"Bill, are you there?"

"I'm here." Silence!

"Bill?"

"Yeah. Tell me again!"

I did, and this time his response was, "I'll call you back."

The next morning, he called. He said that he had spoken with the chief pilot and our stories didn't quite match. Oh, what a surprise!

He told me that he had been instructed to fly the next several trips with me for further evaluation. I surely didn't need another fiasco flight. He assured me that this was no big deal. Not too worry!

I wasn't so much worried as pissed off that I just didn't walk away in Aspen or Pueblo. If the next trip proved a repeat of the last, that was precisely what I intended to do.

66

THE SHARPEST CAPTAINS ARE THE EASIEST TO WORK WITH!

Several days passed during which an introductory meeting was held with all the department pilots formally welcoming me to the Aviation Department. Surprisingly, the chief pilot was very gracious and complimentary in his introduction. He seemed nice enough; he just couldn't fly.

It wasn't long before Bill called advising me that in a days' time, we had been scheduled to fly several company executives and their families to Aspen, Colorado.

I was to oversee managing the entire flight, i.e., preflight inspection of the aircraft, catering, fueling, flight planning, weather reports, and aircraft performance.

He would be available to help if needed and, oh yeah, I was also to fly the trip. After my last experience, I felt some trepidation.

I was confident of my abilities, but so far, Bill was an unknown. If he was anything like the chief, this was going to be an interesting trip indeed. I needn't have worried. Bill was a company man for sure, but also a nice guy.

However, he was somewhat *anal* about things. During the flight, I was given a small bound manual of company SOPs (standard operating procedures). These were written and established by him with the blessing of the chief pilot. He was the second pilot hired by the company three years before and held some departmental power.

He expected perfection from how far the seatbelt buckles should extend over the front of the passenger seats while straightening the cabin to how many Cokes and other assorted drinks should be stocked and how many and what type of sweeteners should be in the galley drawers.

He did have a proven system of loading baggage in the Hawker's small baggage compartment. Watching him load a tremendous amount of baggage in the small forward baggage compartment was amazing, to say the least.

Approaching Aspen, I mentioned once again the Aspen flight with the chief pilot some days before. I thought I was careful not to be derogatory. Apparently, not careful enough, Bill interrupted my interpretation of that flight admonishing me, "The chief pilot is my friend."

I took his meaning. I lightly glossed over my experience and ended the conversation. Being a new hire is difficult. Being a new hire and having a bad experience with the boss—much more difficult. Adjusting to the political winds in the department would require some effort.

The weather was clear with light winds for our approach and landing at Aspen. Slowing the aircraft with early configuration changes while still several miles from the runway allowed for an unhurried descent into the valley.

The landing was smooth, using only half of the available runway after gentle braking. What a difference from the last time.

Bill was very complimentary. I didn't know what he had been expecting, but I don't think he was expecting that.

The return trip to Indianapolis required a fuel stop. Stopping again at Pueblo was Bill's choice.

This time a legal and safe takeoff was made with runway to spare. I couldn't help wondering if the same tower controller was working that day.

Flying with Bill proved a pleasure. He was sharp, skilled, and safe. The contrast of my last flight was amazing.

Flying Vagabond

67

WELCOME TO THE MOVIES!

Soon, the Viper-powered Hawker gave way to a brand-new Hawker 700 model.

Flying the Hawker 700 was a pleasure. It was a bit underpowered but a nice move up from the much older 400 model. Faster with *fanjet* engines and a more modern avionics suite, I soon found myself quite at home after a five-day familiarization and recurrent class.

Not long after, assigned as trip captain, I was on my way to Los Angeles with the chairman as he pursued his new interest: movie making. We were scheduled to spend a week in Los Angeles.

Several days passed when I got a call inviting us to the chairman's movie production offices in Beverley Hills. I was informed that we were to meet *Humphrey Bogart* and *Gene Tierney* at the chairman's request.

"Say again," I said.

In a calm, sincere voice, the invitation was repeated.

Being a bit of an old movie buff, I said, "Humphrey Bogart died in 1954." Gene Tierney died much later in 1991.

"So, you were led to believe," I was told. "Please arrive in one hour's time."

The line went dead.

Calling my crewmate, I relayed the message. He told me I was *full of shit!*

"I'm telling you, that was the message. I guess we will find out soon enough." I said.

Ten minutes later, we were on our way.

Arriving at the production office in Beverly Hills, we were greeted by several very attractive young ladies who were manning the reception area. Introducing ourselves as the boss's pilots, we were treated as arriving *royalty*. Given a tour of the offices, we were told that *Mr. Bogart* and *Ms. Tierney* were currently in a meeting and would be out shortly. Kathy, the young lady conducting the tour, was strikingly beautiful.

Like thousands of other beautiful young ladies in Hollywood at that time, she was hoping for an opportunity in the movies.

What better way than to work for a successful movie producer. I gathered that she felt the boss's pilots just might be a good resource to pursue. Sensing this, I intended to be helpful in any way I could.

The meeting over, out walked *Bogie* and *Ms. Tierney*. I swear, they looked so much like the real people that if I didn't know better, I would have sworn it was Bogart and Tierney.

Bogie had been obviously briefed that the pilots were there to meet them. *Bogie* walked over to me, held out his hand and said, *Hello Eddie* in unmistakable Bogie speak. It *was* Bogie!

The voice, the mannerisms, were spot on.

Ms. Tierney offered her hand and quite demurely whispered, "So pleased to meet you, Eddie." I was blown away.

It was Robert Sacchi and a young Michelle Phillips.[34] They were cast in "The Man with Bogart's Face." Made in 1980, it was a bit of a *turkey* but still made the boss several million.[35]

---

[34] Michelle Phillips along with Cass Elliot, John Phillips, and Denny Doherty were known as "The Mamas and the Papas."

[35] Other movies were: *Porky's* (one, two and three), *Love at First Bite, Zorro, The Gay Blade* both starring George Hamilton and *The Stunt Man* starring Peter O'Toole (an Academy Award winner), among others.

68

EXPERIENCE IS A HARD TEACHER. FIRST COMES THE TEST, THEN THE LESSON!

I departed the following day for Indianapolis, Indiana with 'Bogie and Ms. Tierney,' accompanied by George Hamilton and Cheryl Tiegs the model.

They were to be eye candy for a new shopping mall opening in Indy and were the guests of honor at the opening party held the next evening in the new mall.

Departing late in the evening for Indianapolis, the weather wasn't very good. A squall line was rapidly approaching from the west. A fuel stop was ruled out. Several airports we considered but all were under some shitty weather. With a full load of fuel, my intentions were to nonstop the flight, stretching our range while employing a long-range cruise setting, arriving with a barely legal reserve fuel load.

The weather radar gave off a multi-colored glow lighting the cockpit as it painted several thunderstorms in all quadrants. Picking our way through the worst of it in light to moderate turbulence, we began our descent toward Indy. Passing through flight level 230 (23,000 feet), the number two "HYD LOW" pressure light illuminated followed immediately the by number one "HYD LOW" light illuminating. A dual hydraulic failure?

This wasn't supposed to happen. We only had two hydraulic systems, and it appeared they had both failed. There are procedures to follow in such cases. Before employing those, I immediately lowered the landing gear; an immediate knee-jerk reaction hoping that not all the hydraulic fluid had leaked. The aircraft was not exceeding maximum gear speed due to our altitude. Thankfully, the landing gear deployed. Confused and surprised, my copilot asked, "Why did you do that?" I had no good answer.

There was no published written procedure for that *knee-jerk* procedure, but it worked. There is a provision to lower the landing gear on the auxiliary hydraulic system, but it required about 50 pumps of a hand pump, which now was unnecessary.

The nose wheel steering was a victim of this failure and now would require the use of the rudder pedals for steering commands on the ground. No big deal really, we still had normal brakes with anti-skid[36] protection and should be able to use differential braking to assist with steering commands.

The weather had deteriorated to very low ceilings with the bloody squall line.

The 9000 feet long runway was wet with constant and heavy rain.

"Declare an emergency! How are we doing with the checklists?" I said.

"Hydraulic failure checklist completed. The approach check is in progress."

"Okay, I'm planning a zero-flap approach and landing, as we would have to pump the flaps down. I don't want to do that in case of a go-around. We would need to pump them back up." I was stating the obvious.

---

[36] The Hawker aircraft traps 2300 psi for normal brakes during a hydraulic failure in *most* cases.

"Hawker 62 MS Indianapolis tower, wind 270 variables at 18 knots peak gust 32, cleared to land."

Somewhere inside the final approach fix, the hydraulic gauge, which had been reading 2300 PSI reserved as a safety feature for normal braking, fell to zero pressure.

Emergency braking was all we had to stop the aircraft, and this was going to be dicey, as we now lost our anti-skid protection.

We crossed the landing threshold at 150 knots or so. Steering only with rudders, the aircraft became more challenging to keep to the center of the runway as we slowed.

The emergency brake handle was commanded to the *emergency* position when the speed and kinetic energy dissipated to about 80 knots. Gentle braking brought the crippled aircraft to a safe stop on the runway.

A tug was called, and we were towed to the parking ramp. Everyone had been sleeping in the back of the aircraft, and no one was aware that there had been a problem. Had it *gone south,* Bogie might have *died* again.

This was a new aircraft. How could that happen? It wasn't long before we found out.

Flying Vagabond

69

IT'S A GOOD LANDING IF YOU CAN STILL GET THE DOORS OPEN!

Maintenance soon had the aircraft repaired. They mentioned that both hydraulic pressure switches had incredibly failed and one of them sprung a leak, leaking all the hydraulic fluid into the belly of the aircraft. This can't happen but did.

Two days later, the aircraft was back in the air, once again to Los Angeles, returning the movie types to their homes.

Bill was the captain. Landing at LAX was uneventful. Refueled, he immediately took off for Carlsbad, California to pick up several waiting passengers.

Upon lowering the landing gear while on approach to Carlsbad, the left main landing gear did not extend. Recycling the gear failed to extend the recalcitrant landing gear.

Reverting to the auxiliary system, it still wouldn't budge. Several attempts later, a satellite call was made to British Aerospace with our company maintenance conferenced in.

Unable to arrive at a solution, Bill was advised to return to LAX (Los Angeles Airport) and make an emergency landing.

Of course, LAX tried to get him to go elsewhere not wanting to take a runway out of service. Garrett Aviation was at LAX, a

Hawker service center. He had to land there. With the left main landing gear retracted and the nose and right main landing gear extended, a landing was executed. The left wing was damaged in the landing as the aircraft slowed and the wing dropping to the runway.

Raised and placed on a wheeled skid, the aircraft was towed to a maintenance hangar where it was placed on jacks. The landing gear was finally lowered after much difficulty using a hydraulic *mule.* [37] On close examination, the hydraulic fluid was found to be contaminated. This caused a hydraulic blockage on the left main landing gear uplock release mechanism.

Upon hearing of the hydraulic failure in days prior, British Aerospace refused to honor the new aircraft warranty stating we, *the company*, must have contaminated the hydraulic fluid when replenishing the system after the failure of a few nights before. Our company's attorneys immediately became involved. The contaminated fluid was sent to two independent aviation laboratories for analysis. Sand and bits of neoprene rubber were found in the fluid.

The findings: the neoprene was consistent with aircraft seals, the sand, however, after analysis was found to be from only one place in the world: *The White Cliffs of Dover!* They, of course, are in England, the place of manufacture of the aircraft. *The Brits paid!*

---

[37] A hydraulic mule is a term for an auxiliary device providing hydraulic pressure outside of the internal aircraft system.

70

THE MOST PAINFUL STATE OF BEING IS REMEMBERING THE FUTURE

—Soren Aabye Kierkegaard.

As time wore on, and as the company became wealthier, its mission requirements expanded. A new 50,000-foot aircraft hangar had been built that now housed two Hawker 700s and one model 400F (fanjet engine). After a couple of years, the Hawker 700s were sold, and the company went shopping. Two Canadian Bombardier Challenger 601s were the aircraft of choice. The Hawker 400F was retained. The flight department had grown from six pilots to 12, and soon we all were introduced to international flying. Berlin to Bangkok and all points in between became routine.

The chief pilot had a rough time qualifying in the new a/c. As previously mentioned, he just wasn't a very skilled pilot, especially flying sophisticated swept-wing aircraft. He did eventually qualify with additional instruction. My first trip with him as captain in the Challenger was, to say the least, *memorable*.

The weather was marginal for a successful landing. We were executing a full instrument approach to the west runway at Pittsburgh's Alleghany County Airport during a rather heavy snow shower. The runway was sighted right at minimum approach altitude. Rotating the aircraft for landing while still about 30 to 50 feet in the air, we overflew most of the runway.

The wing on the 601 Challenger is referred to as a *supercritical* airfoil designed to provide maximum lift even at slow speeds. You must literally fly the aircraft—wing—all the way to the ground.

In my experience, I learned that the Challenger doesn't easily tolerate a higher than normal landing flare, and if so, a long runway is most desirable.

"Go around," I said as he resorted to *pumping* the control column trying to find the runway.

"GO AROUND!" I yelled just as the aircraft touched down. He applied reverse thrust immediately along with heavy braking. We were now committed to the landing.

The snow shower, while heavy, was of a light powdery consistency which, when applying maximum reverse thrust caused an immediate *white out* in forward visibility blowing the snow forward of the aircraft.

I knew we were very near the end of the runway. This was not a place you want to be at AGC (Alleghany County) landing to the west as the runway ends with a rather sheer drop of several feet.

At this point, we were along for the ride. When the aircraft finally stopped, and thrust reverse stowed, I had to lean forward to see the end of the runway and the runway end identifying red lights. Turning the aircraft to clear them would be a challenge, to say the least. The runway, or what remained of it, was slick. I took over the throttles literally *backing* the aircraft away from the precipice using reverse thrust gingerly. Not an approved procedure, however, this was the only conceivable way to extricate the aircraft safely. There was no argument from the left seat. He was visibly shaken, and that familiar twitch seemed to bounce around his cheek with its own rhythm. I flew the return trip. This was the last trip I ever flew with the man. It was, however, not the last trip he flew in the aircraft.

71

DUMB AND DUMBER

It wasn't too long before the company realized that our new international flying capabilities required the need for more pilots.

One of them selected was a young fellow with low flying time, a fresh face, a pleasing smile, and a willingness to learn, or so I thought. He would be *broken in* on the Hawker, later advancing to the much more sophisticated Challenger. I shall refer to him as *Dumber*. His first name began with a D. The chief pilot's name also began with a D. Let's just call them *Dumb and Dumber*.

Soon, it was discovered that *Dumber* seemed to be having a few problems. His ability to conceptualize as well as his judgment skills were either absent or suspect, to say the least. Complaints of his performance began to circulate.

Dumb was the fellow responsible for his hiring. He decided this new young fella just needed to be challenged a bit more, sending him to Montreal for training in the Challenger aircraft. Well, *Dumb* had been promoted to his level of incompetence. Why not promote *Dumber* as well? This is sometimes referred to as *the Peter Principle*.

It wasn't long after his training that complaints were once again beginning to accumulate to the point where many captains refused to fly with Dumber. Dumb decided to fly a trip with him to give him the benefit of his *vast experience and aeronautical knowledge.*

The *blind leading the blind* comes to mind. What was soon to unfold with the retelling leaves one completely dumbfounded!

A trip to the Denver International Airport was selected. The passengers for this trip included the chairman of the board, executive vice-president, and the president of sales. The president of sales was himself an active pilot owning and flying an old military T-28 trainer. He was a veteran fighter pilot with several combat hours' worth of experience.

The fight to Denver was uneventful arriving at Combs-Gates FBO on schedule with a planned stop of about three hours.

Sometime later, a call was received advising the crew that the passengers were 20 minutes from arrival at the FBO. Things were made ready; fueling had been completed.

The arriving passengers boarded, door secured, engines started, taxi clearance was received to taxi to the departing runway. Dumb was at the controls with Dumber reading taxi checklists.

As the aircraft was approaching the correct taxiway, Dumber suddenly blurted out, "Turn left here. Turn left here," rather urgently.

Dumb, taken entirely by surprise, did as he was instructed, taking the aircraft...*onto a service road*. Realizing it was a bit narrow and paying no attention to the warning signs stating the obvious, Dumb continued taxiing slowly until being confronted with a service truck at their 12 o'clock position, the driver jumping from his vehicle, waving frantically for them to stop. The main landing gear of the aircraft was just barely on the narrow hard surface.

Realization setting in, Dumb selected full reverse thrust attempting to back the aircraft to the ramp from which it departed. This action practically lifted the service truck driver off his feet.

Bob, the president of sales, was out of the seat and into the cockpit to see what was happening. He was incredulous, advising Dumb, "Stow the reverse and ask for a tow.

"A little—a lot—of embarrassment is better than damaging the aircraft," he said.

Ignoring the advice, Dumb continued *backing* the aircraft and upon reaching the ramp, applied full braking, halting the rearward movement of the aircraft and thus almost tipping the aircraft on its tail, ergo, the prohibition of using reverse thrust to *back* the aircraft.

The reversing of engines from a standstill is expressly forbidden having been employed by me at Allegheny County Airport several weeks before out of necessity and then gently and carefully. Dumb was anything but gentle as reports later had it.

Bob mentioned in the retelling of this story that Dumb had a very serious *twitch* causing his right eye to appear to open and close uncontrollably. Hearing that, and being familiar with said *twitch*, I had no doubt it was true.

Dumber, in the meantime, was stammering: "I looked up from the checklist and was confused as I thought you were about to pass your taxiway," which was about 50 feet further on. *Dumb and Dumber!* It sounds like a good movie title.

The takeoff was normal to the relief of everyone. Sometime later, while airborne, the chairman, already upset over the previous incident asked, "Where is the coffee?"

It seemed that while Dumb had been schmoozing with the girls at the FBO. He failed to notice that Dumber had left the coffee pot that he had taken inside to replenish the coffee for the aircraft.

My question, "So Dumb, how's this evaluation working out for ya?"

The blind leading the blind indeed!

72

DON'T TRUST NOBODY AND DON'T DO NOTHING DUMB!

After several years, the founder and chairman of the company was beginning to back away, gradually giving greater control to his older son. The son, in his 30s and a recent Columbia graduate, became vice-chairman.

Seeing the Aviation Department with its three aircraft and 12 pilots, the son announced the Aviation Department was much too large. There were too many pilots and too many airplanes. Four pilots and one aircraft must go. The Hawker was immediately offered for sale.

I received a call to report to the now director of aviation's (Dumb's) office. He had promoted himself to that new position several months before, installing Bill as the new chief pilot. Asking if I had a pop-up trip to fly, I was told there was no trip. "Just get to the airport."

This was unusual, but I feared this was the future that I have been remembering, my last day with the company.

I knew I had not violated any policies, nor had I done anything wrong. I sure had a bad feeling, however. When I arrived, I wasn't proven wrong?

A meeting was in progress in the director's office.

Advised to, "Have a seat and wait your turn," was a rather interesting phrase wondering whose turn it was before mine.

It didn't take long to find out. The door opened and out stepped Bill with a very sour look on his face pointing to me while making a throat-slashing gesture with his finger. He had just been fired. So much for being the chief pilot and Dumb's friend of many years.

Gruffly called into the office, Dumb wasted no time. I was terminated effective immediately. The reason given was the Aviation Department was experiencing a cutback, and I was part of that cutback. Reminding him of my many years' good service did little good.

"Four pilots and the Hawker are going, and you are one of the pilots."

Mentioning once again I had been a loyal employee for close to 15 years, I explained that I was at a loss as to why I was chosen to be laid off. Of course, I knew this was retribution, as the man simply did not care for me and never had.

"We are doing this fairly," he said "Bill, who has been with the company for 17 years, has just been released, and you who have been here almost as long, are to follow. Two others who have been here less than two years will also be laid off. Two off the top; two off the bottom." Great logic.

"You have one hour to gather up your personal belongings, clear out your desk and vacate the premises. I need your airport pass, your hanger pass, ID card, etc. Any other company equipment or material in your possession is to be placed in one of the boxes that have already been placed at your desk."

I was wearing a sports jacket and slacks. Noticing the company logo lapel pin stuck in my left lapel, he said, "I also want that lapel pin!"

That's when I told him to go fuck himself and walked out of the office.

73

THE GREATEST DANGER IN FLYING IS STARVING TO DEATH

—Earl C. Reed

Finding oneself unemployed after almost 15 years of steady employment was quite a shock. Even though I always thought it might come to this, I was still unprepared and at a loss as to how to proceed.

After a brief spell of self-pity, I remembered of course, that I had been looking for a job what I found this one. I immediately started networking once again. A few days later, I received a call from a fellow who claimed to be with K-C Aviation of Dallas, Texas.

After a few pleasantries, he told me that he knew of my situation and was prepared to offer me a 10-day opportunity flying as a contract pilot for one of their clients. "Would I be interested?"

"I am very interested," I said.

"The trip commences from Van Nuys, California in just a few days. You will be spending the first night in Miami. The next day you will be leaving for Paris. A prepaid American Airlines ticket will be waiting for you at the ticket counter tomorrow morning. It will be one way to Dallas. You will be met and driven to our facility at Dallas Love Airport. We are all anxious to meet you."

This all sounded good, but before I would commit, I asked, "I need to know the contract rate that you are offering."

"Yeah, I'm sorry. I should have mentioned that right off the top. Our client is offering $1100 a day plus all expenses. Are you still interested?"

"Yes, I am. Looking forward to meeting you tomorrow."

It looked like I wasn't going to be starving any time soon.

74

FLYING, LIKE LIFE, IS FULL OF PRECLUDED POSSIBILITIES. CAN'T DO... WON'T DO... SHOULDN'T DO!

Arriving in Dallas, I was driven to K-C Aviation at Dallas Love Airport where I met the gentleman I had previously spoken with the day before. Introducing me to the vice-president of K-C Aviation, I was shown into a conference room. My interview covered a review of my resume followed by the signing of several forms. I was asked if I wouldn't mind taking a short check ride in the Challenger 601 aircraft. It was explained that while they were confident of my abilities, they wanted a demonstration of my ability in the aircraft.

Flying a short round robin trip from Dallas to Houston, we arrived back in Dallas. I was handed a one-way ticket to Los Angeles California. Given the name of the aircraft owner, I was told he would be the other pilot. I would be flying right seat and babysitting this new owner who had only recently acquired a captain's rating in the aircraft. This was not at all what I expected.

Often disconcerting, many owner-operators are poor pilots, as their business is their priority, flying their own aircraft an ego-boosting exercise meant more to impress.

One must continually expend effort and study, which is required to truly become a skilled professional pilot. My experience with owner/operators has been just the opposite. This proved to be such an experience

I immediately thought to ask for more money. Given the events that were soon to unfold, I sure wish I had.

Arriving at LAX, I caught the shuttle to Van Nuys where I checked into the Airtel Plaza Hotel. Calling the contact number, I had been given, I was advised departure the following morning would be at 8:00 AM, destination: Miami Florida. All that would be required of me the following morning was to see to the aircraft fueling, catering, and the aircraft walk-around inspection. Flight planning had already been completed, and the programming of the cockpit computers was to be accomplished by the captain upon his arrival. Relegated to junior copilot status, I couldn't wait to meet "El Capitan."

Completing everything requested of me the next morning, I started the APU (auxiliary power unit) all the while wondering if I had not violated or exceeded my authority in any way.

Soon, an entourage of vehicles drove onto the ramp stopping at the door of the Challenger. A total of six people alighted from both vehicles with a tremendous amount of baggage. None of these folks looked as though they might be the long-awaited "El Capitan" when a rather short well-dressed individual stepped from the lead Rolls-Royce vehicle, approached while extending his hand in greeting, he announced, "I am the captain. Call me Prem."

There were five other passengers who were going to be flying with us.

After a few perfunctory remarks, I was instructed to assist in loading the baggage and even though catering had already been put on the airplane, more catering, a good deal more catering, was being loaded into the galley of the aircraft. I learned that one of the passengers was a long-time employee of the captain. Assisting me with the baggage, he introduced himself as the *flight engineer*. Curious about the title, he mentioned that he had indeed been the *flight engineer* on his employer's 707 aircraft for approximately five years.

The 707 had been sold, downsizing to a Gulfstream IV aircraft, which proved unsuitable. He finally settled on this 601 Challenger aircraft. The captain/owner had only recently been type rated in the aircraft, hence my babysitting duties.

He was a Los Angeles businessman of Indian extraction. He apparently had more money than he knew what to do with and was quite fond of the aircraft and aviation. I had seen this combination of businessman/pilot many times. Rarely was it a safe combination, sometimes ending in tragedy. I was immediately on guard.

Flying Vagabond

75

A FOOL AND HIS MONEY ARE SOON FLYING MORE AIRCRAFT THAN HE CAN HANDLE!

The captain's flying of the first leg to Miami, where we spent the night, went smoothly but his lack of experience in the aircraft was evident.

Departure for Europe had been planned for 2:00 PM the following afternoon. This was a bit unusual, as most departures for the European continent were made at 5:00 or 6:00 PM, later in the afternoon to arrive early in the morning due to time zone changes.

Our 2:00 PM departure had us arriving in Europe in the *very* early hours of the morning. This was not a good arrival time at this particular time of year because of potential fog. I had checked with meteorology earlier regarding this trip. Fog was indeed expected over much of the continent due to a stalled warm front primarily on the west coast of Europe.

Take off and climb out was normal and we leveled at 31,000 feet. Smooth air and a glistening sea reflecting an early afternoon sun greeted our maritime excursion. Thoughts of ancient mariners and Spanish galleons left me with a sense of awe and respect for those brave and daring men; whether pirates, merchants, or sailors of the many navies of the era, sailing into the unknown and uncharted seas—some in search of new lands and passages yet unknown, to continents yet undiscovered, others in search only of gold and riches.

We had been flight planned on a *random* route, pretty much straight across the Atlantic to Europe. Reaching flight level 310, I noticed the power levers were set for maximum speed. Even though we carried maximum fuel load for this trip, with the power levers set for maximum speed at an altitude of FL310, we would run out of fuel just short of the continent. I had yet to see the flight plan, as the captain zealously guarded it.

I felt it incumbent upon me, and certainly from a self-preservation standpoint, to mention that with this flight configuration and altitude we would be hard put to make *feet dry*.

"May I please see the flight plan?"

"No," he responded.

"Why?" I asked.

"Because you don't need to see it. I have flown this route many times, and at this altitude. I know exactly what I'm doing."

"Have you done it in the Challenger?" I asked.

"No, I haven't, but I am quite familiar with oceanic procedures and have filed for a *steep* climb to flight level 390 very soon."

"What if they are unable to grant the *step* climb? Just because you filed for a *step* is no assurance it will be issued. We would be wise to operate under that assumption by bringing the power levers back to provide a constant speed of .74 Mach instead of the .80 Mach number we are currently cruising at. Our fuel flows must be reduced *ASAP* in the event the step climb is declined."

"We are fine just the way it is!"

It was at this point that one of the passengers came forward and said, "Your lunch is ready sir."

This turned out to be his valet. The other passengers were his private secretary, chef, masseuse, chauffeur and, of course, the flight engineer/mechanic.

While he was having his lunch, the flight engineer occupied the left seat in the cockpit. Noticing the high fuel flows of the engines and the low altitude, he asked why we were cruising at such a high speed at such a low altitude. I informed him of what I learned from the captain. Alarmed and shaking his head, he said excitedly, "We'll never make it!"

"Yeah, I told him that. He tells me he's done this many times before and he knows exactly what he was doing."

"He did it in a bloody Boeing 707 with enough fuel to circle the globe," he said. "This is bullshit! I'm going to have a talk with him."

"You had better hurry. In the meantime, I'm reducing power and asking for a higher altitude."

As soon as the power levers were slightly retarded to reduce fuel flow and before the engineer could have a talk with him, he came flying up to the cockpit.

"Just what the hell do you think you're doing?" he said.

"You may be the captain, but your inexperience in this aircraft and your insistence on adhering to some fantasy flight plan parameters are going to get us all killed. I for one will not go silently into that night," I said.

The engineer, who had been silent up to this point, spoke up confirming my concerns and offering his support. The captain just sat there with a dumbfounded look on his face, staring at the flight plan in his hand. Everyone, it seemed, had been kissing this guy's ass for so long while he pretended to wear the halo of some super pilot. He simply lost touch with reality.

Due diligence, caution, study, and the willingness to recognize your own fallibility serve one well in aviation. Arrogance, egotism, and stupidity will kill you.

I immediately called Oceanic Radio on the assigned HF frequency requesting an immediate climb to flight level 390. Told to stand by, it was some minutes later when we were informed, "Challenger 601X, unable climb to flight level 390 this time. Maintain flight level 310."

I advised them that at altitude we would be fuel critical at arrival.

"Be advised, Challenger 601X is reducing cruise speed to .70 Mach."

"Challenger 601X understood; stand by!"

After some minutes: "Challenger 601X your request for cruise speed .70 Mach has been approved. Maintain cruise speed .70 Mach."

I rogered them. Hell, that wasn't a request. I was setting it approved or not.

The captain, staring out of the window, said, "I have always gotten the step climb in the past."

Whether he had or not was immaterial. It is an unlikely and unsafe premise, especially flying oceanic routes, that what one files in the flight plan, and what one hopes for, are always under the watchful eyes of the deep-water fairies.

By this time, the fuel that we had squandered was going to make our Paris destination problematic.

Performing some quick calculations regarding fuel, our best option was to land short of Paris on the coast in either Nantes, France or perhaps Cardiff, Wales. The oceanic controller advised us that the entire French and Welch coast was under dense fog and due to remain so. The exception was Cardiff, the visibility of which had been fluctuating slightly.

"Challenger 601X what are your intentions?" they asked.

"Stand by Challenger 601X."

Being closer to Cardiff now, I called Stockholm radio on HF (high-frequency radio). "Could you read us the last three hours' meteorological reports for Cardiff?"

They indicated that the visibility had been fluctuating between one-sixteenth of a mile and three-quarters of a mile visibility. The forecast, however, indicated slight improvement expected over the next hour. This would coincide with our arrival time over Cardiff.

Nantes was zero/zero in fog and forecasted to remain so for the next several hours and out of the question. Cardiff, our only option, would see us landing with minimal fuel.

"Stockholm radio, Challenger 601X unable to reach Oceanic on channel 13. Please relay Challenger 601X intentions landing Cardiff."

"Challenger 601X, Roger your destination changes."

Entering British airspace, we were cleared direct to Cardiff. The controller, being aware of our situation, read the latest Met report for Cardiff.

"Sky obscured, one-half mile visibility in fog, wind calm."

One-half mile visibility wasn't great, but it sure beat a zero/zero landing. Contacting Cardiff approach control, we were cleared for a full ILS approach to Cardiff.

A full approach meant we could not expect radar vectors to the final approach, but instead had to perform our own navigation for the instrument approach to the airport. This required a turn outbound away from the airport, complete a procedure turn (course reversal) and then proceed inbound to the runway. Not only would this be time-consuming, but it would also be fuel consuming. The captain was flying and seemed to be trembling. Not only did I notice that; I also noticed that he now had a slight twitch or spasm in his right cheek. It sure reminded me of someone. We arrived over the final approach fix for the runway with approximately 1000 pounds total fuel. Five hundred pounds each wing (approximately 75 gallons) and when viewed on the fuel gauges probably gave me a nervous twitch in *my* right cheek, truth be known.

We did not have enough fuel for a missed approach and another attempt at landing. This was do or die. I insisted the approach be made with the autopilot engaged.

We didn't see the runway until about 100 feet. The autopilot was switched off, and a normal landing was made. During the rollout, the captain kept repeating; "We're okay. We're okay." Indeed, we were—no thanks to him.

We refueled and flew to Paris Le Bourget airport. The weather was better by a little away from the coast. Two days later, we flew to Rome for a few days, then on to London, all uneventful. After a few days, we departed with a destination of Van Nuys via Keflavik, Iceland, Gander, Newfoundland and to Bangor, Maine where we cleared customs for our reentry into the U.S. The fear of God had been thrown into the captain, as we uploaded full fuel and each one of those stops along the way, from Bangor to Teterboro New Jersey and then on to Van Nuys, California. I had never been so happy to see Van Nuys. I was handed a cashier's check, shook hands all around and was told a one-way ticket to Indianapolis Indiana, my home at the time, would be waiting for me the next morning at the LAX American Airlines counter.

I was thanked for my service, and with that, he climbed into the backseat of his Rolls-Royce, thankfully never to be seen by me again. I checked into the Airtel Plaza Hotel for a well-deserved rest.

76

EMPLOYED WITH A COMPANY THAT TREATS YOU WELL, PAYS YOU WELL AND TRULY RESPECTS YOUR SKILL AND PROFESSIONALISM, CAN BE BLISS. THE OPPOSITE, HOWEVER, CAN BE PURE HELL!

During the absence of my latest venture, I had received a message to call a company based in Chicago Illinois that had been looking for a Learjet 35 pilot.

Their preference was for a pilot with multiple approach and landing experience into Aspen, Colorado airport. Would I please call at my earliest convenience? I called immediately. Invited for an interview, I drove to Chicago the next day.

Shown into a large conference room, I was introduced to the chairman of the board, the vice-chairman of the board, the company comptroller, and executive vice-president. A review of my resume followed by an extensive interview lasting 45 minutes to an hour after which I was hired as the newest Learjet 35 captain. The company operated two Learjet 35s, one based in Van Nuys, California, the other, Chicago, Illinois. I was the fourth pilot in the flight department.

The company had substantial real estate holdings in Chicago and in Aspen/Snowmass, Colorado as well. All moving expenses would be paid for my move to Chicago, a move they hoped would be rather forthcoming. In the meantime, I was off to Wichita for recurrent training in the Lear.

After training, I began flying several scheduled trips into Aspen, Colorado, the primary destination for this company. The company executives spent a good deal more time in Aspen than in Chicago. I suggested that I move to the Aspen area, as so much time was spent there, in lieu of Chicago.

It took the chairman all about 90 seconds to agree. A few weeks later, my wife and I found a lovely home in Glenwood Springs, 30 miles north of Aspen. It was to be our home for the next several years.

Soon, I was flying international trips to Europe as well as domestic.

Although capable, the Learjet was hardly the correct aircraft for nonstop trans-oceanic flight, if for no other reason than fuel range. Flying frequently to Europe in the Lear soon would become problematic. The chairman and his party would be flown to JFK airport, where they would board the Concord. Calling ahead to British Airways on their operations frequency, advising our ETA and passenger names, we then were given a gate assignment next to the Concorde. British Airways representatives would meet the passengers escorting them up the gangway, disappearing into the beautiful supersonic machine. Sweet deal! Their luggage would then be flown to London in the Learjet. The passengers would arrive in London in less than four hours. We would arrive the next day. These trips became increasingly more frequent, as the company had offices in London.

After several months, I was called to a meeting in the company's main offices in Chicago where I was informed I was now the chief pilot. Quite surprised at the change, I asked what had happened for him to make such a decision? All he would say was, "It was time to make a change." "Congratulations!" As time would prove; a very mixed blessing!

Flying Vagabond

77

YOU START WITH A BAG FULL OF LUCK AND AN EMPTY BAG OF EXPERIENCE. THE TRICK IS TO FILL THE BAG OF EXPERIENCE BEFORE YOU EMPTY THE BAG OF LUCK

During the next year, the company acquired an Astra Jet. A somewhat ungainly looking aircraft on the ground, it was, however, a nice flying aircraft, with one exception. When flown above 300 knots, the cockpit noise became almost unbearable. Being an early serial number with many mechanical issues that were not noticed or found on the pre-buy inspection, we also experienced many delayed or canceled trips during the early months of operation. One such issue occurred on a memorable trip during a steep descent into Denver's Centennial Airport.

It was two weeks before Christmas. Informed I wouldn't be needed for at least two weeks, I was enjoying the downtime, taking in the splendor of crisp Colorado mornings, fast-moving streams burgeoning with trout, cross-country skiing while taking in the snow-capped splendor of the Maroon Bells and Mount Sopris. My first officer, a Chicago resident, was sent home for the holidays. It had been snowing for several days when I received a call.

"Ready the aircraft immediately for a trip to Centennial Airport."

Two of his guests, Highland Ranch residents, a suburb of Denver, needed to return home immediately, as they had an emergency, explaining the Eisenhower Pass was closed due to snow and impossible for them to drive.

"I have no first officer," I said.

"Find one!"

Calling Aspen base operations, I ordered the Astra out of the hangar and would they please have a de-icing and fuel truck standing by. Mentioning my crew member problems, Trish, a young lady who was a fixture at Aspen airport for many years and who knew everyone, gave me a number to call.

The young man who answered assured me he had several hundred hours in the right seat of Astra aircraft. Arrangements were quickly made for him to proceed immediately to the Aspen airport.

The passengers were waiting when I arrived. They were an older couple, and the lady was crying uncontrollably.

Quickly fueling and de-icing, we were immediately on our way to Centennial Airport.

The weather was clear and visibility unlimited on the front range, the snow having stopped there hours before. The Centennial ATIS (meteorological report) was received mentioning the north runway was in use with calm winds, requiring us to fly past the airport entering the final approach leg on a northbound heading as we approached the airdrome from the northwest. Contacting Centennial approach control, we called the airport in sight and were cleared for a visual approach to the north runway.

Ten seconds later, the controller asked us if we would like to land to the south to expedite our landing. Answering in the affirmative, we were cleared for a visual to the south runway. This required an increased rate of descent to prevent the aircraft from exceeding 250 knots below 10,000 feet, as required, the speed brakes were deployed. Immediately, the aircraft rolled rapidly left. It took both of my hands on the yoke to keep it from completely going inverted. We had rolled approximately 140 degrees.

As I attempted to retract the speed brakes with my right hand, the aircraft rolled further left into an almost inverted position. Grabbing the controls, and holding them tightly against the overbank, I yelled to my new first officer to retract the speed brakes for me, as I was sure we had a split speed break problem. He asked, "Where are they?" Oh shit!

The rate of descent was now extreme with the airspeed warning horn sounding as the aircraft oversped in the descent. Letting go of the controls with my right hand to quickly retract the speed brakes, the bank instantly increased to near inverted. Thankfully, the speed brakes retracted, and the wings brought once again to level. Arresting the rapid rate of descent, we continued to Centennial Airport for an uneventful landing. I am not sure how or why the passengers hadn't noticed the earlier unusual attitude. It was later I discovered their only son had been killed that morning in a horrific traffic accident. In their grief, they noticed only one another. My heart went out to them.

Offering thanks, they boarded a prearranged limo driving off alone in their anguish.

As they departed, my *first officer* (I use the term loosely) had disappeared into operations. Upon returning, he announced he had booked a return flight from Denver back to Aspen on United Airlines.

He said, "There is something wrong with that aircraft, and I ain't getting back in it."

I couldn't blame him really. It turned out, he was a trust fund baby from an extremely wealthy family in Aspen whose family friend owned an Astra. I discovered much later he had occupied the right seat in his family friend's Astra as a friendly gesture but had never been checked out in the aircraft as a working crew member. He was a light airplane pilot unschooled in jet aircraft.

I was able to contract with a bona fide Astra captain through the auspices of Combs-Gates aviation at DIA, returning with me to Aspen, I provided him an airline ticket on United, returning him to DIA. An Astra tech rep was flown into Aspen finding the problem several days later.

78

THE HIGHEST ART FORM OF ALL IS A HUMAN BEING IN CONTROL OF HIMSELF AND HIS AIRPLANE IN FLIGHT, URGING THE SPIRIT OF A MACHINE TO MATCH HIS OWN

—*Richard Bach, A Gift of Wings*

Early in the spring my wife and I had planned a long weekend tent camping trip along the Crystal River just west of Carbondale, Colorado.

The first day we were to go camping, a pop-up trip developed. Dispatched to Chicago with guests of the boss, we were to *deadhead* (sans passengers) the aircraft back to Aspen.

I told the wife, "Set up the campsite. I will be returning in a few hours and meet you there."

It was a beautiful day to fly, the sky a magnificent blue marked with fluffy white tendrils marking the passage of high-flying fast movers, destinations unknown.

Returning to and descending into the Aspen area, I canceled our IFR flight plan (instrument flight rule) and descended visually toward the campsite on the Crystal River. Certain the wife had arrived sometime before and was awaiting my arrival, I planned a surprise announcement of my return.

Locating the campsite at our 12 o'clock position and about five miles, I closed the throttles and dove the aircraft toward it. Arriving over the campsite approximately 300 feet above the trees and at a high rate of speed, I pulled the aircraft into a maximum rate of climb adding full power to the engines. The campsite was in a boxed canyon requiring a steep climbing turn to avoid the rock-faced ridge at our 12 o'clock. As the engine noise reverberated in the valley, it announced, "Honey, I'm home!"

Landing Aspen, I drove to the site only to see my wife arriving just ahead of me. She had been delayed. I felt it prudent to forego mentioning my previous airborne antics.

While unloading the camping gear, a fellow camper approached, introduced himself, and mentioned it was a shame we missed the earlier airshow that some *asshole* performed over the top of the site.

"Scared the hell out of the wife, kids, and dogs. I tried to get the number of the aircraft but was unable.," he said

"Oh, too bad," I said.

"Yeah, too bad," my wife said, shooting me a look that withered my dither.

79

"NEMB ME IMPUNE LACESSIT!" NO ONE PROVOKES ME WITH IMPUNITY!

I had been with this company for several years. The last few had been a special challenge. The chairman had divorced his long-suffering wife of several years and was on the prowl for new companionship.

Several ladies stepped up for a shot at this wealthy mogul, most being shot down after a few romps in the hay, a few blowjobs while airborne to exotic destinations and several expensive baubles. He was a miserable man becoming increasingly difficult to please, screaming at every perceived slight or miscalculation.

The straw that broke the camel's back, or should I say, *my back,* occurred while on final approach in a blinding snowstorm to Colorado's Centennial Airport the same airport of my earlier near demise.

It was a cold, blustery day in Chicago. A cold front was rapidly approaching from the west. Dispatched in the Astra to Denver's Centennial Airport with the chairman and six other passengers, a high-level meeting, planned months in advance, was to take place at the FBO—Combs-Gates Aviation. Several more Denver businessmen awaited our arrival at the airport. A conference room had been set aside to accommodate for this significant meeting.

The airborne catering for this flight had been ordered by the chairman's secretary arriving at the airport one hour prior to our proposed departure time. A standard fruit tray, vegetable tray, with assorted breads, cold cuts and spreads for sandwiches intended to be eaten by the chairman and his subordinates during flight. It had been ignored, that is, until the most inopportune moment of the flight.

The chairman's secretary, advising this trip was *do or die* regarding a multimillion-dollar deal in the works for several months, stressed the importance of our timely arrival at Centennial.

The weather at our arrival at Centennial was 100 feet overcast with one-quarter mile visibility in heavy snow. The runway, while plowed, was covered in compacted and drifting snow. The wind favored the north approach and was 30 degrees off the runway heading to the right.

The snow, falling all day, was not forecasted to cease for several hours. The weather was below our legal landing minimums. However, recognizing the import attached to this meeting, I decided to attempt a *look-see* ILS approach.

Intercepting the final approach course and descending on the glideslope, there was a rustling of catering trays in the galley behind the cockpit. The chairman chose this time to peruse the catering.

Asked to please be seated, as we were on final approach, he ignored the first officer's request, stepping forward with the large vegetable and cold cut tray in his hands, screamed in my ear; "What the fuck is this?"

We were inside the final approach fix in rough air and icing conditions, on a very tight instrument approach. Both my first officer and I advised him of our position and would he please be seated, as we were quite busy. Ignoring our request, he slammed the tray onto my arm, the power levers, the center console, and our laps. I was incredulous. The aircraft was still several hundred feet above landing minimums as I calmly asked for flaps to be reset to the takeoff position while adding full power, commanding the landing gear to be retracted.

"Advise the tower we are missing the approach, proceeding to DIA" (Denver International Airport).

Suddenly, staggered back toward the cabin due to our rapid climb, the chairman, recognizing we were not landing at Centennial, began screaming for me to land the *fucking* airplane. Ignoring him, we proceeded to DIA where the weather was more favorable.

Speaking loudly to be heard over the diatribe directed to the cockpit, I advised him a limousine had been ordered to drive him and his party to Centennial.

I doubt he recognized the reason we missed the approach was due to his aberrant behavior and temper tantrum. Too bad really. Always willing to accommodate if possible, my intentions had been to land at Centennial to facilitate his important meeting. Now: *Fuck him!*

It was while diverting to Denver International, picking tomato slices, lettuce, cold cuts, mayonnaise, and bread off me, the aircraft controls and center console, not to mention the mess on the first officer's lap, that I decided to leave this maniac's employ.

Upon landing, the passengers were loaded into the limo. Receiving a call sometime later, the chairman demanded I deadhead the aircraft to Centennial and pick them up for the return trip to Chicago. Telling him, I would check the weather at Centennial, and if good, I would be there. If not, they could expect to return to Denver International via limo. In a raised voice, he told me to get my ass to Centennial immediately. Once again, I told him I would call him back when I had the latest weather report.

At this point, I didn't care what the weather was. I had made up my mind I was not going to Centennial. They were just going to have to limo back to Denver International. Not a vindictive person, as a rule, my stained trousers, the tiny tomato seeds sticking to my sweater, the gooey mess of mayonnaise, mustard and ketchup that was the cockpit, brought my generally good nature, to the breaking point.

"You fuck with me, I fuck with you," I thought.

As it turned out, the weather was just barely at legal landing minimums at Centennial. I made the call advising him I still could not land because of weather.

"I will have the aircraft ready upon your arrival at Denver International for our trip back to Chicago."

He was yelling as usual as I promptly disconnected the call.

Both the first officer and I fully expected to be fired upon our arrival in Chicago. I sincerely was hoping that would be the case, as I had had enough abuse.

There was a definite chill in the air upon his arrival but not a word passed between the chairman, me or my first officer during the entire return trip.

The return trip to Chicago proved uneventful. Once the aircraft was brought to stop on the ramp, the chairman simply deplaned and drove off in his Ferrari.

My years with this company, though financially rewarding, soon proved beyond stressful and began taking a toll on my physical well-being. Being worn very thin by his uncontrolled anger, I recognized I had to take some action. His rantings often left me shaking, not with fear but rather rage at his tirades toward my crew and me. During several years of this abuse, I could barely pass a first-class medical due to my ever-increasing blood pressure.

In fact, had it not been for an understanding medical examiner who I had known and been examined by for several years, I never would have passed. The examiner didn't cheat but would make me lie down for several minutes taking my pressure again when resting.

I then always passed. He advised me to get away from this guy ASAP.

Flying Vagabond

80

ONE PROBLEM IS A PROBLEM, TWO PROBLEMS ARE A HAZARD; THREE PROBLEMS CREATE ACCIDENTS

While in Chicago for extended periods, I took up residence at the Lincolnshire Marriott, in Lincolnshire Illinois, just a stone's throw from the Palwaukee Airport where the company aircraft was kept.

A week passed since the Centennial trip and not a word from the home office regarding my employment. Repeated calls to his secretary to get a *read* on my employment status provided no answer. During this time, I had been waffling between quitting or not quitting. My salary was excellent with year-end bonuses in the thousands.

This would give anyone pause. Some things, however, just aren't worth money. One problem was the constant abuse, the second problem was deterioration of my health, and the third problem was loss of self-esteem and self-confidence.

All led me to a decision to leave before an accident decided my fate for me.

Making the decision took some soul-searching, but I was determined to call it quits. Before I could request a face-to-face meeting with the chairman, the phone rang advising me that in one weeks' time I was to fly him and his new girlfriend to Los Angeles where they were to catch the airlines to Phuket in Thailand.

After dropping them in Los Angeles, I was to fly the aircraft to Aspen and await their return to Los Angeles, where I would meet them, flying them back to Chicago.

This was fortuitous. I planned to arrive at LAX, then advise him of my decision to leave his employ. This would be the last trip I was to fly for him. I would take the aircraft back to Aspen but would not be able to meet him at LAX upon his return or fly him back to Chicago. This plan would get me back to Aspen.

The day of the Los Angeles trip arrived. Introductions were made to the new girlfriend who seemed overwhelmed with his Ferrari, corporate jet and the trip to Los Angeles and Thailand.

During letdown into Los Angeles, I advised him a limo was in place and waiting on the ramp.

I also mentioned, "It is imperative that I speak with you before you leave the airport."

He asked, "About what?"

I told him we were in close to LAX and almost on the approach. It would have to wait until we were on the ground.

Sitting in the back of the limo with him while his young lady visited the ladies' room in the FB0, I gave my notice mentioning my plans to return his aircraft to Aspen.

True to form, in a raised voice and his usual abusive manner, he said, "You'll regret this decision, as no one would pay you the money I have over the last several years."

Questioning my reasoning, I told him he was not a very nice person, and no one had ever treated me with such a lack of respect and belligerence as he had.

My health was becoming an issue while working for him and no amount of money was worth losing that.

With that, I stepped out of the limo with him screaming after me, "You'll be sorry," as his new young lady, returning from the restroom, witnessed his continued tirade. I wonder what she thought as they drove off.

I took him completely by surprise. He drove off before he thought to prevent me from flying the aircraft back to Aspen.

Repositioning the aircraft back to Aspen was certainly helpful in getting me home, but had he prevented me from flying the aircraft back to Aspen, I simply would've bought a ticket on the airlines using the company credit card to get home.

My first officer was Chicago-based and airlined home from Aspen. I have never been so relieved to be unemployed in my entire life.

Flying Vagabond

81

ONCE BITTEN, TWICE CAUTIOUS!

Arriving back in Aspen, I broke the news to my long-suffering wife (number two). She, of course, had noticed my mood swings, snapping at her for no apparent reason. Recognizing the constant pressure that I had been under and the fool I was working for, she was almost relieved to hear the news.

Sad because our life in beautiful Glenwood Springs, Colorado might be ending, we were both equally confident that a new opportunity would soon present itself. Low and behold, it did and within a week.

Determined, and feeling I brought a lot to the table in terms of experience, I made my first networking call to an old friend in St. Louis. Explaining that I was once again seeking work, I asked, did he know of anyone that may be looking for an experienced captain. I couldn't have made a better call! He mentioned not one but two job opportunities that he knew of. One in Denver, captaining a Challenger 601, and one in Hilton Head, South Carolina captaining an older Hawker 700 model. He supplied me with contact telephone numbers for both opportunities.

I was type rated as a captain and experience in both aircraft. Assumed the Challenger opportunity to be the employment of choice, offering not only better pay but continued residence in Colorado, I called the Challenger contact number in Denver.

An interview was scheduled the very next day. Airline reservations were made to Denver and then on to Hilton Head, South Carolina, to check out the Hawker opportunity. A four-hour window was planned for the interview in Denver, hopefully allowing time to catch our flight to South Carolina.

We found our way to the office building in downtown Denver for the interview. Waiting in the reception area, a man approached extending his hand. He introduced himself as the owner of the company. I introduced myself and attempted to introduce my wife.

I said, "This is my wife!"

He would have to have been deaf not to have heard me. He abruptly turned on his heels ignoring her outstretched hand and said, "Follow me," leaving us both surprised. Rude to say the least.

Entering his spacious office, he immediately began questioning my systems knowledge of the Challenger 601. I found this rather odd, as most prospective employers would be more interested in my resume, aviation experience level and goals, personal and family life. If either party showed interest, remuneration would eventually be discussed. None of these things were mentioned. Instead, I was given an oral examination of the systems of the Challenger presenting in-flight situations requiring immediate attention asking how I would address these situations.

This was not only bizarre, this was: "Son of Bizarre, Part Two."

During these discussions, I asked what had happened to his previous captain. He told me nothing had happened to him—yet! He was waiting to hire his replacement. This did not sit well with me.

I asked him why and how long his captain had been with him. Not willing to divulge his reasons, he told me that the man had been with him for five years. He then suggested that I drive to Centennial Airport where his aircraft was hangered. There, I would meet a young lady—his flight attendant, who had been in his employ for 10 years and, "Is a trusted member of my employee family."

She would be expecting me. With that, he stood, shook by hand, walked me to the door and said goodbye.

During the drive to Centennial, my wife asked me what I thought about working for this individual. She expressed that we perhaps would not have to move from our home in Glenwood Springs if I accepted employment here in Denver. I reminded her Glenwood Springs was 190 miles to the west of Denver and that we might indeed have to move to Denver should I accept the job.

I also mentioned I wasn't keen on accepting the job, describing in detail what I thought about this man's character. I didn't think much about it at all.

The aircraft was indeed beautiful, and so was the flight attendant. She was a lady of about 42 or 43 who spoke very highly of the owner. She softly asked me not to mention that I was there in pursuit of employment as a captain on the aircraft, as the *about to be replaced* captain was nearby. I asked her if the captain knew he was about to be replaced.

Shaking her head negatively, she said he didn't, adding she felt rather sorry for him. I felt sorry for the whole bunch of them.

I was in the hangar for all of about 20 minutes when I said, "Thank you very much for your time. It was a pleasure meeting you."

With that, we drove to the airline terminal in Denver awaiting our departure time to Hilton Head, South Carolina. I didn't want anything to do with this man or his company. His ethics spoke volumes about his character and his inability to ever garner my trust. Leaving one bad situation, I was not about to get into another. A week later, this man's representative called to say I had the job. I turned it down.

Flying Vagabond

82

THERE IS A TIDE IN THE AFFAIRS OF MEN WHEN TAKEN AT THE FLOOD, LEADS ON TO FORTUNE

—Julius Caesar

Hilton Head Island was delightful. The current Hawker pilot met us. He explained that he had a commercial pilots license with a commercial Hawker type rating. He owned a small Beechcraft Baron aircraft. The owner, on discovering he was a pilot, sent him to Flight Safety to acquire his Hawker type rating after an older Hawker 700 model had been purchased.

Discovering quickly he was in over his head, he asked to be relieved of his pilot-in-command duties on the Hawker, and in fact, wanted nothing more to do with the Hawker. Smart man! The decision to replace him was made only one week before I was told of the opening.

Timing is everything. His copilot was a novice airman who had no formal training in jets let alone the Hawker.

Arrangements had been made for my wife and me at the Hilton Head Weston hotel on the island. A dinner meeting was scheduled that evening with the owner and his family.

Greetings exchanged, drinks and casual conversation ensued in a very relaxed and pleasant atmosphere.

The owner was one of two founders of a software company called i2 Technologies in Dallas. They were both of Indian extraction. He and his partner had started the company only a few years before and now were worth an estimated one billion dollars each. Asked later what i2 meant, he jokingly responded *Two Indians*. It really meant, Intelligence Squared. In speaking with this man, I was immediately put at ease. His gentle manner, quick wit, and soft, rather high-pitched voice were winning me over big time.

One thing I did notice, however, was that he never removed his straw Panama hat. It wasn't long before I discovered the reason.

When the conversation finally got around to whether I may be interested in going to work for him, he explained that he was undergoing treatment for brain cancer. Already having undergone one operation and chemo, he would understand if I were to reconsider employment. The Panama hat had been hiding a very nasty scar across the top of his head.

I asked if he would be amenable to a three-year contract. He readily agreed, asking to outline my terms, stipulating salary and benefit requirements, all of which would be presented to his corporate attorneys for their review.

These conversations took place privately on a deserted hotel patio overlooking the Atlantic Ocean. He did ask my salary requirements. I responded with a rather high figure, to which he readily agreed. Rarely does this happen without negotiation.

Having discovered the training of my new first officer had been nonexistent, a condition of my employ was a full initial Hawker Jet training course for him and a recurrent Hawker class for me to be conducted at Flight Safety. Extending his hand, he said, "Welcome to my family, Hilton Head Island and hopefully a long and prosperous association."

Within two years, he was gone.

Those two years proved wonderfully transformative for me. I grew to love this man very much. He was the kindest, most life-loving and sincere individual I had ever met.

He greeted and treated everyone with dignity and respect. I miss him terribly to this day. His name was Kana. He answered to Ken. He was truly a gentleman who could also be wonderfully naïve at times.

One such time occurred when arriving at Teterboro Airport in New Jersey. He was scheduled for a procedure at Sloan-Kettering Cancer Institute the next morning.

As he climbed into the limo, I wished him a nice evening and closed the door. I stepped back into the aircraft to finish some paperwork when my co-captain said:

"Hey, I think Ken is still here. Wonder what's wrong."

Sure enough, the limo hadn't moved. Stepping down from the aircraft, I opened the door asking, "Is everything all right, Ken?"

He said, "Everything's fine. I am just waiting for you guys. When you're ready, then we'll all go to dinner."

That was a surprise, but that is who he was, just a sweet man.

Several minutes later, we were all in the limo on our way to the lower east side of Manhattan where Ken's limo driver had made reservations for us.

The driver, I'll call him Fred, said, "Now Ken, remember what I told you about this place. It is frequented by *wise guys* so please don't stare at anyone. The food is the best in Manhattan, the wine even better and the ladies are all beautiful but keep in mind this is a rough neighborhood with a rough crowd. You're gonna love it!" I had the distinct feeling that wasn't just meant for Ken.

The limo stopped outside of a nondescript building with no signage, just a well-lit doorway with stairs leading to the second floor. Fred explained even though there was no signage, the restaurant was well known and well attended.

At that, he called our attention to several very high-priced vehicles, Rolls-Royces, Bentleys, and Mercedes-Benz parked within two blocks of the entrance. Many of these, he explained, were bulletproof.

While Fred parked the limo, we helped Ken up the stairs.

Ken gave his name, and we were immediately seated at a large table in the bar area explaining there would be a small waiting time for the main dining room. Handed the wine list, Ken immediately asked for a specific wine circa 1974. It was a *Château* something or other.

The young lady assured Ken with such an extensive wine collection, it may take some time to locate a bottle. Several minutes passed. Returning with the bottle in question, she presented it to Ken.

It was quite dimly lit in the bar area, which presented a problem in reading the small print on the label. Agreeing to a taste, he took a sip, swishing it around in his mouth, he said, "Man, that was good but, do you have a 74?"

The waitress looked stunned. Looking at the label more closely, it was revealed it was a 1976 *Château*. She apologized and disappeared.

We all were equally stunned by his discerning palate. They did have a 74, and we enjoyed three bottles of it at $1500 a bottle.

The bar area was quite large, filled with dark complexed men with impeccably groomed black hair, wearing dark suits accompanied by beautiful women. Many of the men appeared to have slight bulges under their arms.

Ken, enjoying himself immensely after several glasses of very expensive wine, became a bit more vocal, asking Fred, "Who did you say comes here?" rather loudly.

Fred, leaning forward indicating for Ken to keep his voice down, softly said, "*Wise guys.*"

"Oh yeah, wise guys!" Ken said louder than necessary.

At that, 15 or 20 of the people closest to our table turned and glared in our direction sending chills up our spine. Fred was motioning frantically for Ken to keep his voice down. Ken's back was to the bar, so he saw none of this asking for a clarification, "Who are the wise guys?"

Fred, leaping across the table and gently grabbing Ken by the arm, pleaded with him to keep his voice down.

I couldn't tell if I was more embarrassed or more frightened. I was sure I just wanted to be somewhere else at that moment—a fond memory of my friend, Ken.

Flying Vagabond

83

ONLY THE GOOD DIE YOUNG!

While on a trip to Cincinnati where Ken was to give a speech to General Electric executives, he received a phone call shortly after landing. It wasn't good. Sloan-Kettering advised him the results of his last round of tests showed his cancer had returned. Further surgeries were not an option. They informed him he had two months to live at the most.

As I entered the hotel room, the phone was ringing.

It was Ken. "Please return to the airport. I need to go home immediately," he said.

When we arrived at the field, he was waiting in his limo by the aircraft. He apologized for the rush but explained that he had just received some *bad news*.

It was while we were en route to Hilton Head that he told me his news. My heart sank! Why do the good have to die so young? We were both the same age at the time.

Several months before, Ken had asked what the fastest corporate jet was. The Citation 10 was the answer, and, after doing some homework and conversation with Cessna, he ordered one.

He said, "I really like my Hawker, but it is just too darn slow and old."

Two days after receiving the recent terrible news, he asked me to stop by his home explaining he needed to see to his wife's travel needs after he departed. I thought that had been taken care of. He had other thoughts.

Arriving at his home, he wasted no time in telling me to cancel the Citation. His reasoning was, she didn't need such a fast airplane.

"Get her something that will be reliable and safe. It doesn't have to be fast, just reliable."

"How about a new Hawker? They still make them, don't they?" he asked.

I did try to talk him out of canceling the Citation, as he was about to suffer a great deal of financial loss should the order be canceled. He didn't care.

Asking his wife what she thought her mission requirements might be, she replied:

"Nothing exotic, just some domestic flying around the country."

I canceled the order to the tune of 150,000 dollars and ordered a new Hawker XP from Raytheon.

84

"ERRACE EST HUMANUM"
TO ERR IS HUMAN

—Seneca the Younger

Shortly after this time, my first officer quit for personal reasons. I was conducting interviews. After flying with several contract pilots, I settled on a young fellow. Before I could offer him the position, I received a phone call from a pilot explaining that he heard of my job opening and was interested. Explaining that the position had been filled, he simply would not take no for an answer, showing up the very next day on my doorstep. He had been flying for a lumber company in Atlanta, a short drive from Hilton Head.

He practically begged me to give him a shot at the job. I introduced him to my wife and my new *boss lady*. My wife did not like him at all warning me to be careful. The boss lady, however, loved him at first glance. He was her age, fortyish, not bad looking and a smooth talker. I was immediately told to hire him. I explained that I had someone else in mind.

"Forget it," she said.

"Hire him. I like him." I was forced into a very bad decision as time would tell.

The Hawker 800XP and the "money tree" design.

Hawkers aren't all that pretty, but this one was just beautiful. Designing the interior, as well as the exterior, and having carte blanche, I took full advantage of it. My new boss, we called her *B,* which was her first initial, asked, "Will I like it?"

"If you don't, I'll change it," I said.

She agreed, and at the unveiling, she was completely taken in with what I had done. She absolutely loved it. I am confident Ken, her late husband, would have loved it as well.

The instrument panel. The overhead panel was painted the same—
very different. You either liked it or hated it.

The queen's seat. Note the crown: pure 24-carat gold, later
removed to our Falcon 900EX.

Our first trip was to California, the second to Naples, Italy where she immediately bought a Villa in Positano on the Amalfi coast. So much for *a little domestic flying.*

We made many trips across the Atlantic, some of which were a bit dicey returning because of headwinds. I advised that we had the wrong aircraft for this kind of semi-monthly flying.

"I love my Hawker," she said, "What should I do?"

Don't ever ask a corporate pilot that question!

85

CAUTION: AVIATION MAY BE HAZARDOUS TO YOUR WEALTH!

I t wasn't long before I had been tasked with procuring a suitable aircraft that met our mission requirements. Many factors are involved in choosing the correct aircraft for the right mission.

Most corporate pilots begin salivating at the mere thought of a shiny new Gulfstream corporate jet. I was no different.

Based on Hilton Head Island, we were only 30 miles from Savannah Georgia home of Gulfstream corporation. A demonstration flight on a brand-new GV was quickly arranged for the following week to Milan Italy, then on to Naples.

With 14 passengers, baggage, catering, and three crew members, we departed Hilton Head Island's 4000-foot strip at 5:00 AM, rotating for takeoff approximately 2800 feet down the runway. Amazing performance! Eight hours and 35 minutes later we landed in Milan, Italy.

The *Queen Bee,* as we now referred to her, sat in her usual favorite seat, all the way to the rear of the cabin.

Halfway during the flight, I asked what she thought of the aircraft. Much to my surprise and chagrin, she said, "I don't like it."

"I was incredulous!"

"Why?" I asked.

"Look" as she pointed forward.

"Look at what?" I said.

"It's just a big round tube!" she said.

"They are all big round tubes. There are no square aircraft," I said.

"I'm just not fond of it. Find something else."

To say I was disappointed would be an understatement. She was the only one we had to please, so I set about finding *something else*. Money was not an object; her happiness quotient, however, was something else again.

After the GV trip, we set out once again in the Hawker to Naples Italy. Stopping in Shannon Ireland on a technical stop, we happened to park next to a Falcon 900.

"What's that?" she asked.

"A French Falcon jet."

"Do you suppose I could get a look inside?" she asked.

"I am sure we could," I replied.

As we approached the Falcon, the captain appeared in the doorway. Lo and behold it was a friend and former crewmate of mine who I hadn't seen for some 15 years. His passengers had all gone inside to the duty-free shop.

"She's a bit messy inside, as I haven't had an opportunity to clean her up after a long flight from Russia. You're certainly welcome to have a look, however," he said.

She was immediately taken with several windows in the cabin and insisted that it was much wider than the Gulfstream. The Falcon cabin is, in fact, a total of four inches wider than the Gulfstream, two inches on each side. I believe that with so many cabin windows allowing so much light into the aircraft, it does, in fact, seem wider.

"Get me a ride in one! I love it," she proclaimed.

I did!

The Falcon at Lake Tahoe.

A flight attendant applicant, with a very "attractive" resume.

Flying Vagabond

86

WHO CAN YOU TRUST!

One of my more memorable trips to Italy in the Falcon was a near calamity.

Departing Teterboro in the late afternoon, the Falcon jet had 14 passengers, a flight attendant and $3000 worth of catering from *Rudy's* a specialized corporate aircraft caterer. Our arrival in Paris was scheduled for early morning. The flight was routine until reaching 30 west longitude, smack in the middle of the Atlantic with approximately 1000 miles to anywhere.

A position report was made to Oceanic Radio when I faintly heard my name called. Thinking it was my copilot, I said, "What?"

He said, "What, what?"

"Didn't you call me."

"No."

Looking back toward the cabin, I was startled, to say the least. Standing all the way to the back of the cabin was our principle lady passenger pointing frantically to the cabin overhead. A fine smoky mist was filling the aircraft.

"Holy shit! Look!" I said, pointing.

Turning to look where I was pointing, the copilot immediately leaped from his seat. Pushing past the flight attendant, I heard her mumbling softly. At first, I thought she had been singing or humming.

Not our usual flight attendant, she had been acquired last minute from ATA Airlines, as our regular attendant's husband was injured in an accident just hours before departure time. Calling a good friend with ATA, he hooked me up with this gal.

She had limited experience with the airline and little to none with corporate aircraft. An extensive briefing and instruction ensued indoctrinating her as best we could. It was all we could do.

As my crewmate pushed past her, I asked, "What are you doing?"

"I'm trying to cook this damn fish for dinner."

Noticing exasperation in her voice, I asked how that was working out.

"Not very well. The damn microwave keeps quitting on me."

"What do you mean?" I asked

"Well," she said.

"When I pressed the on button on the microwave it seemed to work okay for a while then stopped working. The button no longer turns it on."

She went on to say, "I did manage to override it though with a different switch up here."

Pointing to the hinged translucent cover for the circuit breaker panel she lifted the cover. I saw a 50-amp circuit breaker had popped—a very large amperage circuit breaker indeed.

She reached up, held it in, and the microwave hummed to life.

Incredulous at her stupidity, I shouted: "Stop that! You want to kill us all, you stupid bitch?" I was never one to hold back.

She didn't seem to understand the ramification of what she had done. Convinced we found the source of the problem, we now concerned ourselves with the possible consequences of her actions.

A satellite call was made to Dassault Aircraft in Paris. After much transferring, a technical supervisor was reached. Explaining our predicament, answering several questions, he seemed sure the danger had passed but needed to be addressed immediately when landing. He advised changing our destination to Geneva, Switzerland a service center for Falcon jets. I made the decision to deplane our passengers in Paris where we did a thorough walk-around inspection of the aircraft before departing for Geneva.

The tech had explained that he felt sure the cooling fan on the top of the 60-cycle invertor had seized, thus popping the circuit breaker, as it should have to prevent overheating. By holding the breaker in, she had been overheating the inverter to the point that when we finally removed the galley in Geneva to inspect it, the insulation had been burned to the point of becoming very brittle and crumbled to the floor of the cabin.

Crumbling as it did, I shudder to think what might have happened if she had not been stopped pushing that breaker in. Flight arrangements were made, and she was sent home from Geneva. Good riddance! Several thousands of dollars later, we resumed our trip itinerary.

Flying the Falcon was always a pleasure but soon, the globe-trotting that was once exciting, adventurous, audacious, and awesome became monotonous, mundane, and humdrum. International corporate jet flying was becoming more restrictive, challenging and stressful with each passing year.

Flying Vagabond

87

I DON'T SUPPOSE IT'S GONNA FUCKING RAIN

—Joan of Arc

Much time had passed with at least 100 trips to various places in the world. Returning home after having been in Italy for a couple of weeks, my wife and I planned a week vacation to Virginia Beach for a brief getaway. The car was loaded, and just as we were about to depart, the phone rang.

Would I please arrive at the boss lady's house ASAP? This sounded urgent. I arrived soon after and was confronted by two of her money managers. They were the guardians of Ken's money, now his wife's inherited fortune.

There are times when the "F" word is just appropriate. This was one of them. I suddenly, and with no warning, found myself unemployed. Five years of devoted, loyal service was repaid with a "Thanks for your service." I was *Gobsmacked*! In the immortal words of Michelangelo, "You want *WHAT* on the fucking ceiling?" I couldn't have been more stunned.

The reason given was vague at best, indicating at one point that even the airlines retired their pilots at 60 years of age. Denying it was an age issue, they were cautious explaining only that they were looking for a change.

It turned out that my one-time desperate first officer had been bad mouthing me for some time to anyone who would listen, especially the boss lady, to whom he had grown extremely close. I was never given an opportunity to discover what if anything I should defend against, knowing full well I had done nothing to defend. I was simply replaced. Hiring him turned out to be one of the worst decisions I have ever been talked into. Within five years, he was in, and I was out.

My wife has often reminded me of her earlier fears. I should have listened.

Like Joan of Arc, I was on fire. The injustice of this action compelled me to consult an attorney.

"Forget it," he said.

They have the right to do what they want, and they did.

"Sorry, the world is full of bastards."

Yeah, buddy!

88

THERE IS NO PROBLEM SO COMPLEX THAT IT CANNOT BE BLAMED ON THE PILOT

—Dr. Earl Weiner

Soon, I was once again flying a Falcon 900EX and a Falcon 50 for a company located in Tampa, Florida. The chief pilot was a grand fellow whose company I enjoyed very much. The owner of these aircraft, a wealthy Tampa businessman, seemed a nice fellow. Small in stature, large in ego, constantly carrying a briefcase, he would never allow any of us to touch it. I later learned he was a Scientologist and the briefcase held documents of the *church*. He was a substantial contributor to Scientology and an extreme, almost fanatic practitioner of that organization's dogma.

Case in point: his business partner, also a Scientologist, was having difficulty with his wife, a lukewarm practitioner of Scientology. She continually protested the large donations that were expected of the wealthy faithful, continually casting aspersions on the practice and the faith.

He, the business partner, was told she either stops bad mouthing, gets in line as a good follower or he must...*must*, divorce her. She wouldn't; he did. If true, that is getting into one's life in an extreme way. Going to church doesn't make you a good Christian any more than standing in a garage makes you a car. Shades of a cult. David Koresh from Waco comes to mind.

Within a few months of being hired, an FAA part 135 certificate was acquired, and we were now flying charter. I never liked flying charter much, but if you had to do it, do it in a Falcon. Wonderful machines! Many trips around the globe were challenging but rewarding.

During a refueling stop in Tampa, the aircraft was scheduled to take off again for New York. A crew change was to be made with a new copilot who had been awaiting our landing at the Tampa Airport Marriott. Receiving the call that we had landed, he was immediately driven to the far side of the airport where the aircraft was located.

The boss, noticing fueling had finished, asked, "Where is he?"

Told he was on the way and almost at the aircraft, he said, "He should have been here waiting. He's fired; let's go." Incredulous, we started engines as the fuel truck pulled away from the aircraft. We both saw the fuel truck drive away from the aircraft as we started taxiing for takeoff. This was to become an issue several days later.

As many wealthy aircraft owners are, he was one arrogant asshole. Two days after returning to home base in Tampa, the boss received a call from Raytheon Operations (the FBO operator) at the field saying we had run over a fueling hose as it was being coiled as we started taxiing for take-off some days before. They were demanding payment for the damages to their equipment. Confronting each of us separately with the news, I assured him that was not the case, as we both witnessed the fuel truck pulling away from the aircraft before we released brakes. He not only didn't believe me, but he also became belligerent in his accusations. Nothing I could say would sway him, threatening to make us pay for the damages. I remember saying to him out of frustration, "What you don't seem to understand, is that I SAW the truck pull away from the aircraft." This bit of information transfer was greeted with an icy stare as his secretary almost dropped the pen she had been taking notes with. Little did I know that no one told him he did not understand something and those who did, did not survive long in his employ. Oh, shit!...again.

Seeing the fuel truck pull away from the a/c, we think the fueler somehow caused the damage to the hose, feeling he could blame us and thus save his job.

Let me cite an example of how arrogant this prick was.

Stepping up to the cockpit one day on our way to Aspen, Colorado, he struck up a conversation regarding the hurricane threat that Tampa was under at the time.

He said, "I don't know why someone doesn't do something about stopping these things every year. If I were in charge, I would have that problem solved in a week. REALLY! Since light travels faster than sound, some people appear brighter until you hear them speak!"

I always had the feeling I was about to be fired by this guy. It wasn't long after, I was! The Falcon 50 was sold. As the last pilot hired, I was the first to go. A year later, I received a call saying he was found dead at his desk in Tampa—no doubt working on the hurricane problem.

My Tampa-based "rides" on the ramp in Boulder, Colorado.

89

"QUI AUDET ADIPISCITUR"
HE WHO DARES, WINS.

To pass the time when not flying, I applied to The Old Time Trolley company in St. Augustine as a part-time tour guide. St. Augustine being the oldest city in the country, and being a history buff, I thought it would be fun, and I was correct.

I also auditioned at the local community playhouse called the Limelight Theater and, to my surprise, was cast as the lead in the very first play for which I had auditioned. It was called *Greetings*. I was having a blast in my off time from flying. It didn't pay much but added interest and fun to my life.

The author in the driver's seat hamming it up for the camera with a full trolley.

The author in *Greetings*.

Having a "blast" in my off time from flying.

On the set of *You Can't Take It with You.*

90

UNCLE DADDY IS HOME

Flying has been my passion; being away from home and family was the downside. A friend and fellow pilot told me you know you have been away from home a long time when you walk in your door, and your young children start running around yelling; "Uncle Daddy is home. Uncle Daddy is home!" My children were all grown but looking back I missed a lot of significant events in the lives of my children, which eventually led to a failed marriage. This is the curse of many professional pilots. I will forever remain sad and regretful.

After many years in the cockpit, I made the decision to pursue other venues in aviation where my years of experience would be appreciated on the ground. Enter, CAE Simuflite!

Years before, when acquiring my Falcon 900EX captain's rating at Flight Safety in Dallas, Texas, the instructor mentioned he thought I would make a great Falcon instructor. "Call me if you ever need a job," he said.

That had never occurred to me nor did it interest me at the time.

By regulation, I needed a flight proficiency check once a year. One year, returning to Flight Safety for my check, I discovered my old instructor had moved over to Flight Safety's competitor, CAE Simuflite, also located in Dallas. I looked him up and transferred our training to CAE. He was now a training manager. Once again, he expressed an interest in my becoming a pilot instructor. Flying around the globe and enjoying the heck out of it, I sure wasn't interested until one day, I was. I made the call!

Once pleasantries were exchanged, I asked if the offer was still open for instructor employment. I was assured it was and to get a computer in front of me. I was *walked* through the application process and told I would be getting a call in a few days.

Two days later, CAE HR called. After an extensive telephone interview, It was asked if I could find my way to Morristown, New Jersey in a few days. Explaining that Morristown, Whippany, New Jersey was where a new CAE training center had only recently opened; they were actively recruiting pilot instructors. All I knew of New Jersey was Teterboro and Newark airports. Flying into these places was one thing; living near them, something entirely different. I called my mentor.

"Hey, where are you?" I asked as he answered.

"Morristown, New Jersey," was the reply.

"I thought you were in Dallas."

"Been here since they opened the center almost a year ago," he said.

"Well, I think you can forget about me." New Jersey sucks and so do you for not telling me."

"Hey Eddie, it really is very nice here, not at all like you are picturing. I know you are thinking all of New Jersey must be like Teterboro or Newark, but you are wrong."

They call New Jersey the garden state for a reason. Come on up and see for yourself. Bring a few days' worth of clothes. There will be several days of interviews, testing and indoctrination to get you on board. I will be happy to show you around the facility and the local area. Can I count on you being here in a couple of days? I have really talked you up here at CAE and hope will consider the offer."

Sigh. "Well, okay, but no promises. See you in a couple of days."

91

WASHINGTON SLEPT HERE!

Arriving at CAE Morristown at 0800 October 20th, 2008, I was full of trepidation, uncertainty, and anxiety. Of course, I knew what simulator training was all about having suffered through hundreds of training sessions in various aircraft during my flying career. However, I had never experienced being on the *other side of the table* as the instructor. This was going to be different.

Warmly greeted, I was given a tour of the facility after which I was shown into a classroom and asked to take a seat. There were eight or 10 prospective new hires undergoing indoctrination. Somewhat confused, I took a seat after being introduced to the instructor and the other hopefuls. Things were moving fast, very fast! There were no expected pre-hire interviews and no testing. Other than my previous telephone conversation of a few days earlier with CAE HR and the acquaintance of my former Falcon instructor, I was pretty much already hired. The presentation of my pilot certificates seemed to be all that was required to become a prospective CAE instructor. I mentioned to him later I wasn't sure about this at all. His response was, "How bad can it be?" Laughing he said, "Washington slept here," referring to the Revolutionary War era when George Washington made Morristown his headquarters during many campaigns against the British.

The Residence Inn became my home for several weeks. After the first week of *indoc,* I flew home to Florida and packed for an extended stay in New Jersey. As I left, I mentioned to my wife that I would give it six months, after which I would either return to Florida, or we would relocate to New Jersey.

92

I NEVER THOUGHT I WOULD BE AN INSTRUCTOR. NOW I ARE ONE!

O nce they discovered that I had a great deal of flying time in most models of the Hawker aircraft I was selected as a new Hawker instructor, not a Falcon jet instructor. Disappointed but happy to have a job, I stayed quiet and pressed ahead.

The Bae-125, (Hawker 1000) simulator had recently been installed at the Northeast Training Center in Whippany having been moved from the Dallas, Texas CAE facility. Only 52 of this model aircraft were manufactured, and this simulator was the only one in existence for this model.

This simulator was a *convertible* sim in that it could be changed over to a model 800 Hawker simulator overnight. Also, at this facility was a separate flight simulator for the model 800XPi Hawker, which had the latest Pro-Line 21 avionics. Both 800 model designations are HS-125 and share a common captains type rating. The Bae-125 however requires a separate type rating in the U.S. but not in Britain. They are all the same type rating there. The FAA insisted that the differences between models warranted a separate type rating for the larger Bae-125 Hawker.

My initial training completed, I was assigned as a new simulator instructor. I began certifying clients in all three simulators as well as conducting ground school and aircraft systems training classes.

Six months passed quickly. I soon discovered I had an aptitude for this work and was enjoying it. I decided to stay. Assigned new responsibilities as a *lead instructor* or SME (subject matter expert) I protested, as I didn't seek nor want the position. It was and is a rather thankless position with many responsibilities with little or no compensation. It is a pseudo-management position, answering to the training manager.

Simulators were running day and night with heavy client loads. Many of the clients were low-time pilots with little or no jet time. Many of these young men and women and a few older pilots as well, had never been above 10,000 feet in their entire careers. High-altitude flying presented new concepts and introducing them to things such as coffin corner, Mach number, Mach tuck, and high-altitude aerodynamic stall recovery were utterly foreign to many.

Some had been doing things such as *banner towing* over some beach somewhere—a brain-numbing job. Swept-wing jet flying differs as much as beer to 20-year-old single-malt scotch. Getting these folks through the course was challenging to say the least. The transition has been likened to attempting to drink from a fire hose in the short training and transition time allotted. Extra training rapidly became a rule rather than the exception. Many were enrolled in a copilot course where when completed would be well qualified to fly under the mentorship, tutelage, and guidance of experienced captains. Frustratingly, not all would make it.

Then, there were the *experienced* captains. Most were a pleasure to work with; some, not so much.

93

THE FAA DUDE!

A sking me what I thought of this guy is like asking a fireplug what it thinks about dogs!

Let me begin by saying, not all FAA dudes are like the one described below. Most are serious, experienced professionals with a huge responsibility, mandated by Congress to keep the skies safe. Thank God we have them.

Early one morning, upon entering the pre-briefing room, I found two experienced captains waiting to greet me. Meeting each other only a few days before in ground school class, they were assigned simulator training together.

I had been warned by their previous ground school instructor of the recalcitrance of the fat guy with an FAA logo on his hat. He reminded me that every ground school class includes one ass who, at five minutes before 5:00, asks a question requiring a 20-minute explanation. This was that guy.

He was an FAA inspector from southwestern Florida attempting to acquire a type rating in the Hawker 800XPi aircraft. Sixty-something, unsmiling, with a sour expression and a baseball cap featuring the FAA logo perched proudly on his bald head, he begrudgingly extended his limp hand in greeting.

The other pilot from a charter company in the Midwest was a repeat client who was known to me. He was already a holder of a type rating in the aircraft and was upgrading his position to captain. I began my briefing.

Several minutes into my initial briefing, the fed (FAA dude) asked me somewhat sarcastically, "How much time you got in this machine or are you one of them that has never flown the machine and think they know it?"

Having pegged him immediately as an asshole—not all FAA examiners are assholes; most are great people—I assured him I had quite a bit of time in not just this model but many of them. Not satisfied, he said, "Answer my question. How much time you got in this machine?" The other client spoke up saying, "He just told you!"

"I wanna hear it from him."

"Eight thousand plus hours," I said. "Actually, nearer 9000 hours."

"Bullshit! Nobody has 8000 hours in any one airplane."

"Did you come here just to harass me or to learn to fly this aircraft?" I asked.

"I have years of airline and corporate flying experience, and I have never met a pilot with so much flying time in one aircraft. I think you're full of shit," he said.

The other client pilot stood at this time and with a raised voice told him to, "Shut the fuck up and let him do his job."

With his arms folded across his chest, resting on his ample gut, he was at last quiet. When I finished briefing today's lesson plan, the fed said, "You through?"

"Excuse me!"

"Are you through?"

"Yes, I am. Why do you ask?"

"Let me tell you something. I'm gonna go in there and fly this thing the way I want to fly it. There is an old saying in aviation, "Those that can, do. Those that can't teach. You get my meaning?"

"Loud and clear, captain! I can't wait for you to show me how it's done," I said sarcastically.

With that, we entered the simulator.

Now, there are no new ways to crash an airplane, but I swear this guy found a few. Scheduled for a hot day session where the takeoff temp would be a limiting factor, it was destined to be very busy with several in-flight emergencies presenting themselves. The very first takeoff was from Reno, Nevada with Captain America in the left seat. This was conducted on a wet runway.

At approximately 100 knots airspeed, a failure was introduced requiring an aborted takeoff. The aircraft departed the runway.

FAA dude said, "I'm a little rusty." Trying it again, and again, the aircraft left the runway each time. The fourth attempt, after much discussion, proved successful. We departed for San Francisco. The lesson plan called for several emergencies to be experienced enroute: depressurization of the cabin, hydraulic failures, and engine failure, to mention a few. I couldn't wait.

Reaching a cruise altitude of 33,000 feet, I introduced a compressor stall caused generally by a disturbance in the airflow of an engine. The symptoms are often engine instrument fluctuations such as an intermittent high internal turbine temperature accompanied by a banging sound as the interrupted airflow of the engine attempts to correct itself.

FAA dude was at a loss to recognize the symptoms until the engine failed explosively. This was a cause for an immediate emergency descent to a lower altitude to be initiated. Multiple failures appeared because of the catastrophic engine failure including a loss of all hydraulic system pressure and regular brakes to stop the aircraft upon landing. There are procedures to be followed in each of these scenarios with the proper use of checklists accompanied with system knowledge, not the least of which is the lowering of the landing gear employing an auxiliary hydraulic system. FAA dude struggled desperately to fly the aircraft. His co-captain's attempt to help with proper procedures were constantly ignored. The copilot warned several times that the landing gear was not extended and was ignored. After several attempts of this warning, I subtly indicated to the copilot that no further attempts should be initiated regarding landing gear extension. We waited. At a few hundred feet above ground, an onboard warning system sounded: "Too Low-Gear!" Captain America never said a word.

The aircraft crashed attempting the landing at San Francisco.

All hell broke loose in the simulator as the FAA dude turned on me, accusing me of getting even by giving him unrealistic failures. He complained to management.

The training manager assured this asshole that many of the exact same failures he experienced in simulation had, in fact, been experienced by me several years before in the actual aircraft and had been relayed to him by my copilot of that dark and stormy night several months before. The difference: I didn't crash the aircraft.

FAA dude was advised that he would do well to learn from me. Protesting, he asked for a new instructor. He also complained about the new instructor. To the instructor's credit, he continued in his attempts to get this jerk through training.

It took FAA dude several days longer than the average pilot to graduate, but graduate he did—barely. We have never seen him again. Good riddance to him!

94

I HAD TO PROMISE NOT TO DO THAT AGAIN!

On occasion, instructors are called upon to *facilitate* a simulator session for a country's check airman. They will conduct the check ride of their fellow countryman while the instructor operates the simulator.

So it was when I conducted the simulator for the Canadian MOT (Minister of Transport, Transport Canada). The client was French Canadian, as was the check airman. The check ride did not go well at all. The young lad being checked made several serious mistakes that I would have stopped the ride and failed him for, but the MOT guy kept it going to the end. Sure that the client would be failed, we entered the debriefing room. The Canadian check airman told me to wait outside in the hallway. This was unusual, to say the least. After about 25 minutes, the young client who I thought for sure would be told he failed, exited the room with a huge smile. Curious, I asked, "How did it go?"

"What do you mean?"

Curiosity getting the best of me because of the smile, I asked, "Did you pass?"

Becoming defensive, he said, "Yes. Why?"

I couldn't believe it. Reaching into my breast pocket, I retrieved my business card. With him watching, I jotted down my address on the back and handed it to him.

"What's this?"

"My business card."

"No, I mean this," pointing to the backside of the card.

"My address."

"Why do I want your address?"

"'Cause I don't want you flying over my fucking house."

He made a phone call. I had to promise not to do that again.

95

TWINKLE TOES

The differing levels of competence was a revelation. Some client proclivities were strange and sometimes downright weird. Enter *Twinkle Toes*.

A qualified Hawker captain, he always wore flip-flops while training. Not strange enough? His toes, all of them, were painted a bright red. His first officer attested to the fact that he wore them rain, shine, or snow, warm or cold temperatures, wearing them on all flights as well. It was winter in New Jersey with about four inches of snow on the ground when I was introduced to him. At first, I thought it a joke, but no, this was de rigueur for this gentleman. It didn't seem to bother him at all that everyone starred.

Many clients and instructors would sneak a look at this fellow and walk away shaking their heads. How could he not notice the looks from more than a few of his peers? Not bothered, he just carried on as though this was perfectly normal, oblivious to the snickering his toes inspired. He was a charter captain flying to many destinations on several continents. I couldn't help wondering what his passengers and the folks in other countries thought of this.

I also was a bit concerned how he would handle an emergency evacuation of the aircraft, if the need arose, while wearing flip-flops. In an onboard smoky fire, it might be difficult to extinguish between his toes and a flame. Some people's kids!

One of the more memorable client pairs I have had to this day were two Russians whose English was suspect, to say the least. They did not have American licenses. They were experienced pilots with Russian pilot certificates. We—CAE—administer recurrent training to many nationalities without American licenses. These are *training only* clients requiring no testing beyond specific training events.

I noticed that when I would ask a question of one or the other of these two, they would give me a thousand-mile stare, remain quiet, turn to their partner and, while still quiet, shrug their shoulders, prompting me to ask the question another way. Still no success. Facetiously, I asked if they spoke any English, as English is the universal language of aviation.

"Of course," they replied in unison.

"Then why aren't you answering me when I ask a question?"

"Veey dun't know answer," Was their reply.

Oh. Well, why didn't you say so! Many attempts to ascertain their knowledge base left me frustrated and uncertain. We proceeded to the simulator.

They both flew very well and demonstrated that they were safe and professional. However, as I was finishing the last sim session, I noticed the guy flying was having some difficulty with a crosswind landing. They were tired, and I had previously mentioned to them that this crosswind landing would be their last for the day. However, the landing was almost a full stall landing from about 50 feet with the aircraft bouncing and very nearly leaving the runway.

I said, "I know I said that would be the last landing, but we have to do a *tad* more," reverting to American slang, explaining that his landing was wholly unacceptable and would have to be repeated.

Turning in his seat, looking me in the eye, he said in heavily-accented English, "What is tod?"

"Not tod, I said, 'Tad'."

"Who is tad?" he said.

"Not who, tad is a what," I said.

"What is tad?"

"It's an American saying."

"Yes, you are American saying that. I am Russian saying, '*Who* is tad?'"

"Again, tad is a what, not a who. Tad means a little."

"A little what?'

"Look," I said, "It is just a slang expression."

"What is slang?"

Okay, we're finished for today!

There was an exchange in Russian again accompanied by a lot of shoulder shrugging.

Checking their schedule for the next day, I was delighted to see they had a different instructor assigned the following day who wasn't one of my favorite instructors having caused me some grief sometime before. He was a bit of an arrogant asshole. I called him.

"Hey," I said. "Tomorrow you have Ivan and Oleg, the Russian pair. They are doing okay. Oleg's English is good. Be sure to use the term, *tad* as in '*We'll be finished in a tad.*' He really wants to learn to use that slang term. Be sure to tell him it's a *slang* phrase."

The next afternoon passing them in the simulator bay after their session, the instructor said, "You son-of-a-bitch!"

Revenge is sweetest when you can almost taste their tears!

Flying Vagabond

96

A GEM CANNOT BE POLISHED WITHOUT FRICTION, NOR A MAN PERFECTED WITHOUT TRIALS

—Lucius Annaeus Seneca

A great landing in a simulator is a little like kissing your sister. It's just not the same as touching down in an actual aircraft employing the judgment and skill required to accomplish the task successfully, especially with a challenging crosswind, but still rewarding.

Now retired from active flying, I am active as ever in aviation. In my role now as a simulator pilot instructor/check airman, I remain swamped.

Adventure may hurt or frustrate you at times, but monotony will kill you. The challenges faced daily by those of us whose thousands of hours have earned us the right to be called *torchbearers* are anything but monotonous. Interesting, challenging, rewarding, and, at times frustrating, this adventure as a teacher/instructor has been most gratifying. Passing on the skill, *knowledge,* and *wisdom* required to make one a safe and professional pilot, while highlighting the differences between them, has been my greatest source of pleasure.

Knowledge is knowing a tomato is a fruit. Wisdom is not putting it in a fruit salad.

The satisfaction of advancing a young man or woman's career leaves me both humbled and thankful. Progressing through my career, I have learned much from my mistakes. An instructor's knowledge should be proportional to those mistakes. A client/student's failures/mistakes in a simulator training session should also serve them well. Often, however, they affect a client/students' performance negatively, leaving them unable to move past them. An understanding must be reached with the help of the instructor detailing the benefits of self-discovery while embracing the lesson.

Thomas Watson once said, "If you want to increase your chances of success, double your failure rate. Failing a maneuver is an experience. Accidents happen when you run out of experience!" I couldn't have said it any better.

A man was once asked what he wished to be remembered for? His response, "I made a difference!"

There's only the trying. The rest is not our business.
                                        —*T.S. Elliott*

FINIS!

38441311R00210

Made in the USA
Middletown, DE
08 March 2019